DEDICATION

When I was younger my Mom told me the story of the little boy who lived on an island who wanted to give his teacher a gift. He walked several days to the ocean, picked up a handful of sand and made his long walk back home. He gave the sand to his teacher and she commented on how far he had to go to get it. His reply was the Journey was part of the Gift. I see this Book like the Gift... but it's the Journey I wish I could share with you... the countless days of support, encouragement and love from my husband, Trent; my children, Angela, Aimee, Ashley and Aaron, who have made the Journey an exciting adventure every step of the way; and my parents, Eugene and Velta Moe, who showed me the world and all it's possibilities. They taught me to Believe in Myself, in the Gift of painting that God has given me, and to go wherever I allowed my Dreams to take me. This work is a fulfillment of the Dreams and has been a joy to me, but the greater Joy has been in the Journey. 1996 is the year of my sweet Mother's cancer diagnosis. I would like to dedicate this book to her, as my gift offering and to thank her for her Journey. Even if the cancer should take her life, it could never take who she really Is, and has Become, in the process of Life and Living.

May the Journey be full for each of you who find some creative joy from this Book.

ABOUT THE AUTHOR

Tami Christensen started Tole painting over 10 years ago. Her friend, Kathy Garner, taught painting classes and kept asking Tami to join her beginning session. Tami told her she wasn't interested. She had just barely purchased her new serger to satisfy her passion for sewing and wasn't willing to put it aside to take up a new hobby. Finally Tami's resistance broke down. She took Kathy's class and got hooked. Tami put away her serger and sewing machine and has had a paint brush in her hand ever since. Now Tami teaches pianting classes and currently resides in Idaho with her husband of 17 years, Trent, and four children; Angela, Aimee, Ashley and Aaron.

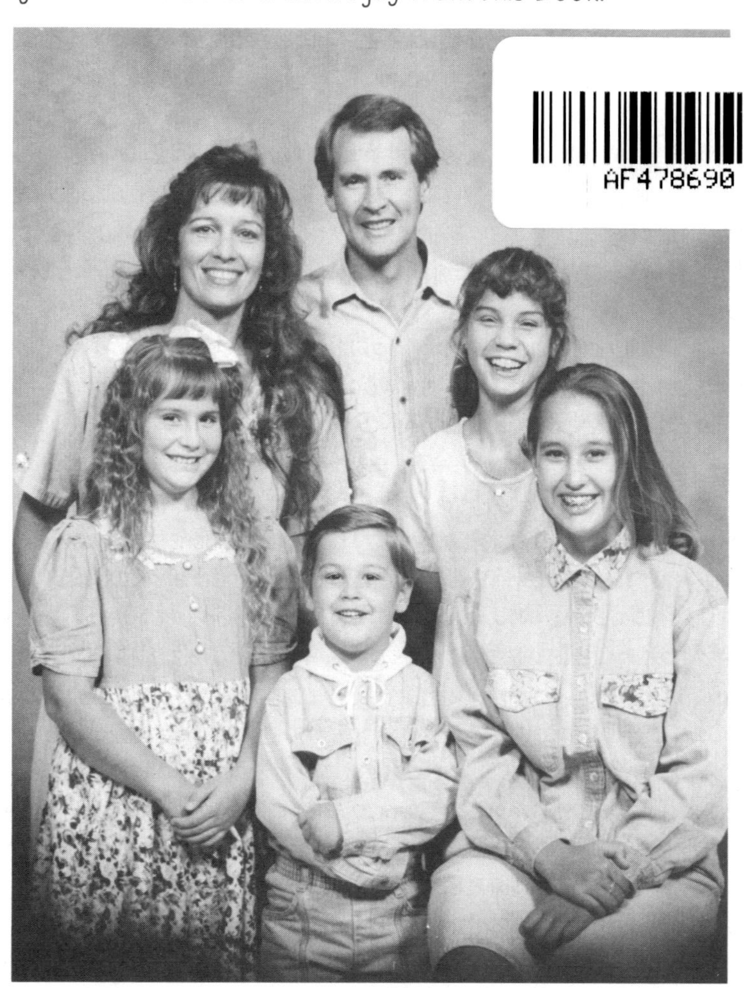

GENERAL INSTRUCTIONS

GETTING STARTED

1. Sand wood using a medium grit sandpaper (i.e. 220 grit).
2. Seal with brush-on water based sealer. This provides a sealed surface so that fewer coats of base paint are needed. Let dry thoroughly.
3. Sand again very lightly using a fine grit sandpaper (i.e. 400 grit).
4. Trace your design onto tracing paper using a permanent black pen (a pencil will smudge). Using transfer paper, transfer your design to your wood.

GENERAL TERMS AND TECHNIQUES

TEA DYEING

To get a more rustic look from fabrics and doilies, soak or spray with regular strength tea. Try experimenting with different brands and strengths of tea to get varying looks. Let dry before attaching to painted project so it won't "dye" your wood piece too.

BASE PAINT

Paint the area with 2-3 thin coats of paint to cover, smoothing out ridges as you go, letting paint dry well between coats.

STIPPLE

(I use a Loew-Cornell White Nylon Fabric Dye Brush No. 8) Dip the tip of dry brush in paint. Using a tapping motion on a paper towel or other absorbent surface, get rid of most of the paint on brush. Then, using the same tapping motion, tap brush onto wood leaving only a hint of color. Remember, the idea of stippling is to give color without having the definite line of regular painting.

SPLATTER

Dip an old brush or toothbrush into paint and run your finger across the bristles. This will make thin specks of paint on your wood. The wetter the brush, the larger and more transparent the specks.

SHADING AND HIGHLIGHTING

The technique is the same for both shading and highlighting. (The only difference is the color you use. Shading will be using a color darker than your base color. Highlighting will be using a color lighter than your base color). The technique is called a "Float" or a "Side-load Float". To do a float, dip your flat brush in water and blot ever so slightly onto a clean paper towel. Dip one corner of your brush into the paint, about 1/2 of the brush, and blend onto palette paper by stroking your brush back and forth until paint looks "soft". The idea is to have paint on ONE side of your brush blending with the water IN your brush and having no paint show on the OTHER side of your brush. **TIP:** When painting a float on your wood, do it in one continuous, smooth stroke. If you stop in the middle of a stroke or paint it with an irregular motion, your paint will look uneven and jagged. The smoother and more even your floats the prettier your painting will be! This is where Delta Color Float can be a lifesaver!

"DOT AND DRAG" TECHNIQUE

This technique is for making easy flowers and leaves. Dip the end of a stylus, toothpick, or end of a small brush into paint. Dot it onto wood and while holding end down, drag it slightly. You can vary the size of flower or leaf by varying the size of brush handle you dip into paint.

LINING WITH A BRUSH

Use a liner brush that is in good repair, no wild Phyllis Diller hair do's on your liner brush! Thin your paint with water to the consistency of ink, rinsing your brush often as you line.

LINING WITH A PEN - Always use a permanent lining pen instead of paint to draw your finishing lines.

WASH

Add water to paint. The more water, the more transparent your color will be.

FINISHING YOUR PROJECT

1. After all the painting is completed, remove all smudges and remaining transfer lines by gently erasing lines with an art eraser or regular pencil eraser. You can also wipe clean with a lightly wet cotton-tipped swab.

2. Spray two-three light coats of finishing spray/varnish. This will not only give a finished look to your project but it will also help protect the colors from fading over time. If you are putting a project outside, I recommend putting several layers of water- based varnish on after the spray varnish to give it extra protection from the elements.

DELTA CERAMCOAT ACRYLIC PAINT

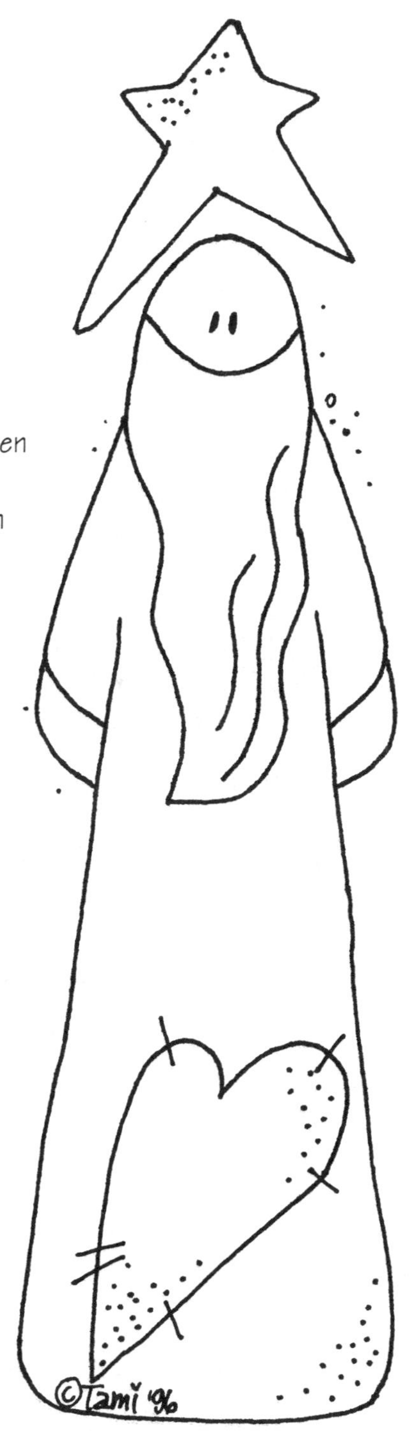

2010 Forest Green	2506 Black
2070 Wedgewood Green	2401 Light Ivory
2101 Butter Yellow	2424 Bambi Brown
2025 Burnt Umber	2464 Sachet Pink
2469 Antique Rose	2505 White
2133 Cape Cod Blue	2463 Cactus Green
2445 Green Sea	2131 Nightfall Blue
2132 Bouquet Pink	2129 Gypsy Rose
2405 Dusty Mauve	2441 Stonewedge Green
2436 Charcoal	2447 Village Green
2455 Blue Wisp	2407 Candy Bar Brown
2437 Rose Mist	2450 Rose Cloud
2470 Taupe	2016 Lavender Lace
2465 Tide Pool Blue	2005 Pale Yellow
2019 Fleshtone	2064 Sunbright Yellow
2042 Pumpkin	2426 Cadet Gray
2456 Dusty Plum	2126 Medium Flesh
2026 Orange	2054 Golden Brown
2443 Napa Wine	2480 Persimmon
2118 Lichen Grey	2422 Leprechaun
2467 Wisteria	2434 Vintage Wine
2045 Fiesta Pink	2078 Straw
2029 Caucasian Flesh	2428 Cayenne
2459 Crocus Yellow	2412 Empire Gold
2022 Light Chocolate	2085 AC Flesh
2433 Island Coral	2425 Territorial Beige
2049 Spice Brown	2435 Trail Tan
2075 Maroon	2107 Tompte Red
2068 Christmas Green	2419 Deep River Green
2001 Antique White	2062 Maple Sugar Tan
2063 Spice Tan	2127 Dark Flesh
2017 Queen Anne's Lace	2453 Wild Rice
2033 Dresden Flesh	2116 Black Green

GENERAL SUPPLY LIST

BRUSHES

Loew-Cornell Red Sable 7300 No. 4 Shader Brush
Loew-Cornell Red Sable 7300 No. 12 Shader Brush
Loew-Cornell La Cornell Golden Taklon 7000 No. 4 Round Brush
Loew-Cornell White Nylon 801-00 Round Brush
Loew-Cornell White Nylon Fabric Dye Brush No. 8
Loew-Cornell Red Sable 7500 No. 6 Filbert Brush
Loew-Cornell American Painter Taklon 4300 No. 6 Shader Brush

MISCELLANEOUS SUPPLIES

Loew-Cornell Brush Tub
Old Toothbrush (for splattering)
Spanish Moss
Cotton-tipped Swabs (a painting "eraser")
Fabric Scraps
Raffia, Natural/Blue/Orange
Wire, 19 Gauge
Hot Glue Gun and Glue Sticks
Palette Paper
Tracing Paper
Battenburg Lace Doilies - Wimpole Street Creations*

Paper Towels
Sandpaper (Medium and Fine)
Permanent Black Lining Pen
Jute, Three Ply
Natural Excelsior
1/2 Inch Cup Hooks
Stylus
Transfer Paper
Paper-crimped Hair

Delta Ceramcoat Color Float
Delta Quik'n Tacky Glue
Delta Crackle

Delta Waterbased Sealer
Delta Spray Satin Varnish

*Look for Wimpole Street Creations products at your local craft store. If unavailable, contact Barrett House, P. O. Box 5840585, North Salt Lake, UT., 84054-0585, (801) 299-0700

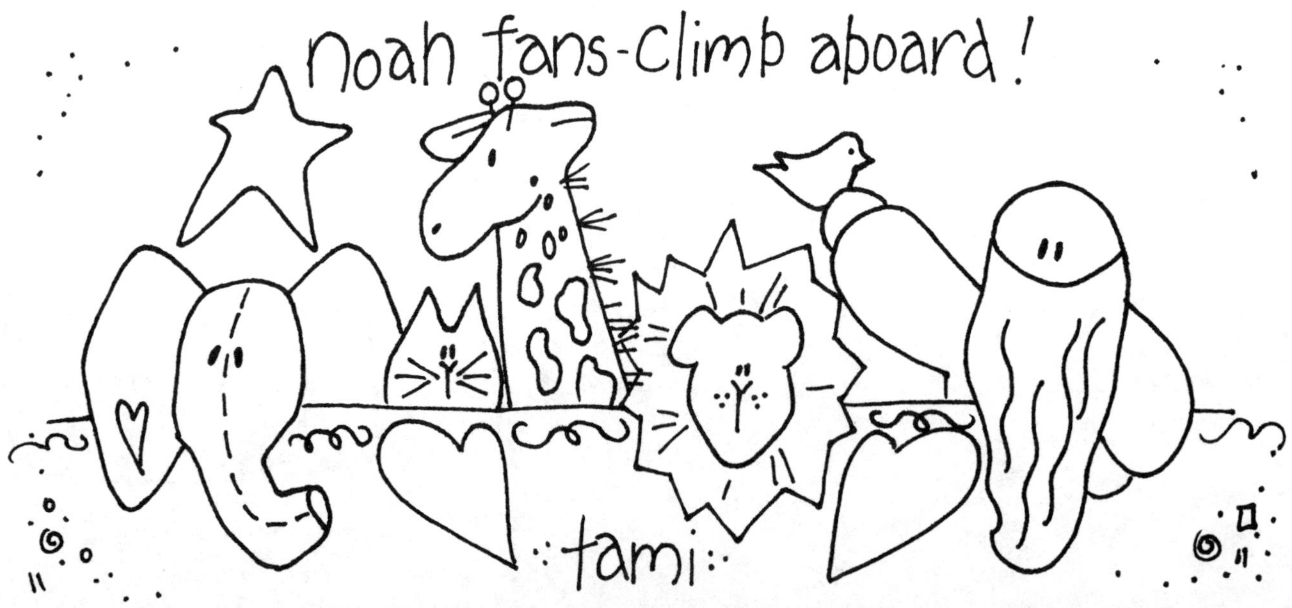

COUNTRY BIRDHOUSE ON STAND

PAINTING THE STAND

1. **Nightfall:** Paint the bottom base piece.
2. **Cape Cod:** Paint the top of stand where birdhouse sits.
3. **Light Ivory:** Paint the post. Lightly splatter top and bottom of stand.
4. **Cape Cod:** Lightly splatter the post
5. Paint the welcome "arm" piece following directions from "Country Welcome Sign."

PAINTING BIRDHOUSE

1. **Light Ivory:** Paint all of birdhouse.
2. **Cape Cod:** Paint the light blue checks on the roof.
3. **Nightfall:** Paint the dark blue checks on the roof.
4. **Dusty Mauve:** Paint the thin lines on the roof. They go in the middle of each check on roof.
5. **Cape Cod:** Lightly splatter birdhouse.
6. **AC Flesh:** Paint bunny angel.
7. **White:** Paint wings.
8. **Bambi:** Shade wings and bunny angel.

PALETTE - Delta Ceramcoat

Nightfall	Light Ivory
Cape Cod	Bouquet Pink
Dusty Mauve	AC Flesh
Bambi	White
Wedgewood Green	

MISCELLANEOUS SUPPLIES

Spanish Moss
Ivy Garland
Fabric Scrap 1" x 5"

ROOF FLOWER

COUNTRY BIRDHOUSE ON STAND Cont.

9. **Bouquet Pink:** Lightly stipple cheeks of bunny angel. Line every other thin line on bunny wings. Paint the cut edge (inside) of birdhouse hole/door. Paint the bottom center block.

10. **Cape Cod:** Line the remaining thin lines on bunny wings. Paint the four remaining blocks.

11. Block No. 1: Paint flower **Bouquet Pink.** Shade left side of flower **Dusty Mauve.** Center heart is **Dusty Mauve.** Leaf is **Wedgewood Green.**

12. Block Nos. 2 and 3 : Paint flowers **Dusty Mauve.** Paint center hearts **Bouquet Pink** and **Dusty Mauve.** Leaves are **Wedgewood Green.**

13. Block No. 4: Paint flower **Bouquet Pink,** shade left side **Dusty Mauve.** Paint center heart **Light Ivory.** Leaf is **Wedgewood Green.**

14. Paint roof flower. Flower is **Bouquet Pink,** shaded **Dusty Mauve** on left side. Center is **Dusty Mauve.** Heart is **Light Ivory.** Paint leaves **Wedgewood Green.**

15. Black Lining Pen: Line/stitch everything.

ROOF DESIGN

dk. blue	lt. blue	dk. blue	lt. blue	dk. blue
lt. blue	Lt. Ivory	lt. blue	lt. Ivory	lt. blue
dk. blue	lt. blue	dk. blue	lt. blue	dk. blue
lt. blue	Lt. Ivory	lt. blue	Lt. Ivory	lt. blue
dk. blue	lt. blue	dk. blue	lt. blue	dk. blue

COUNTRY BIRDHOUSE ON STAND Cont.
FINISHING TOUCHES

Assemble birdhouse together. Screw in hooks to "arm" so you can change hanging designs. Varnish birdhouse and stand very thoroughly with finishing spray/varnish. If birdhouse will be used outside, I recommend using a spray sealer, 2-3 coats, letting dry then varnish again with a brush-on water based varnish. That will give maximum weather, humidity, sun protection to your birdhouse. (Be sure to use a spray sealer first so the pen lines won't run with the brush-on). Glue fabric knot to bunny's ears. Glue Spanish Moss inside birdhouse hole and winding around post. Add ivy garland and glue in place.

SMALL NOAH'S ARK

PALETTE - Delta Ceramcoat

Light Ivory	Cape Cod	Burgundy Rose	Lichen Gray
Maple Sugar	Spice Tan	AC Flesh	Bambi
Nightfall	Dark Flesh	Black	Fleshtone
Gypsy Rose			

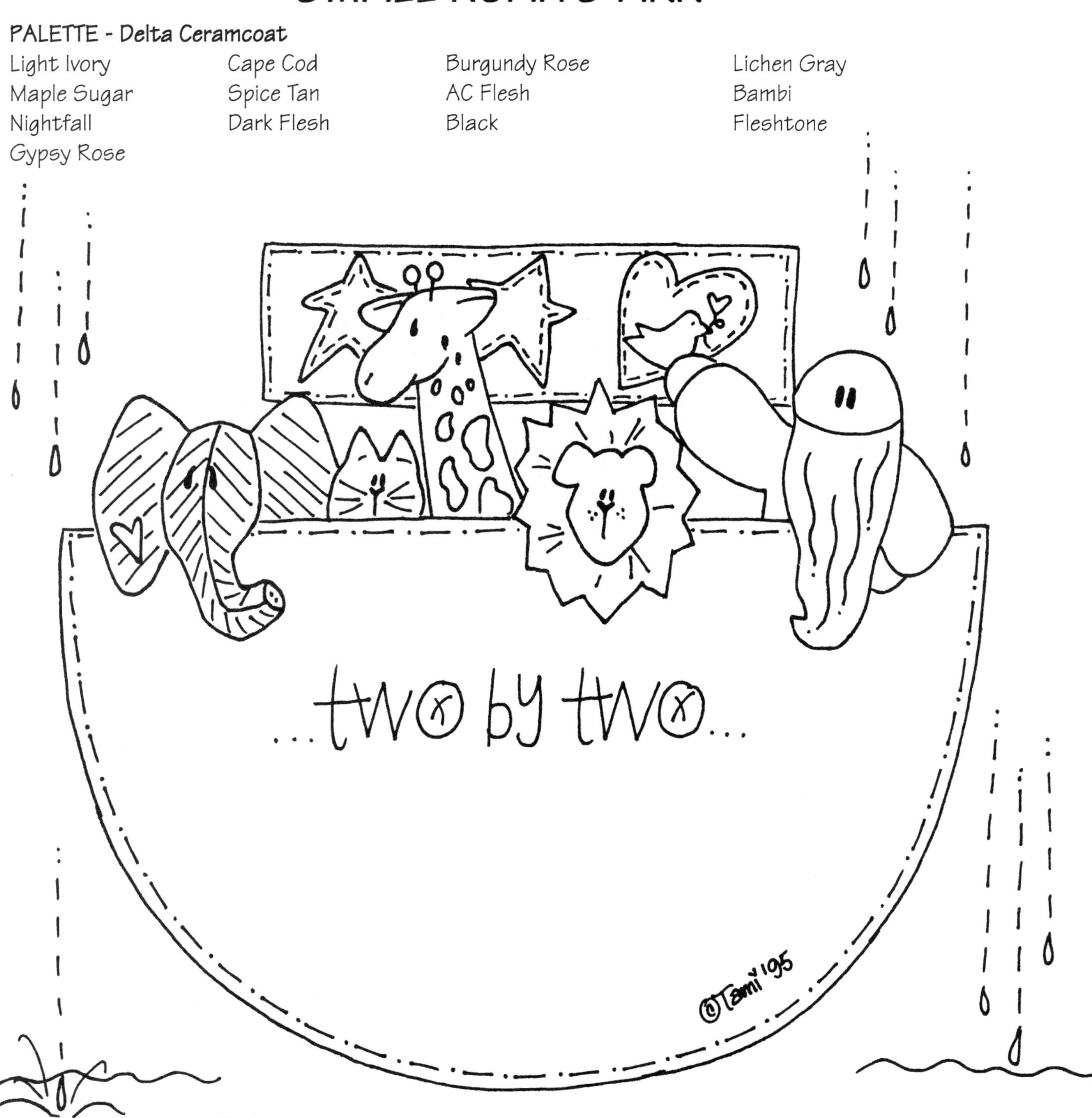

Failure is the only thing that can be achieved without much effort.

SMALL NOAH'S ARK Cont.

1. **Light Ivory:** Paint Noah's beard and heart on Ark.
2. **Cape Cod:** Paint lower section of Ark.
3. **Burgundy Rose:** Paint Noah's robe and right star on Ark.
4. **Lichen Gray:** Paint elephant.
5. **Maple Sugar:** Paint lion and left star.
6. **Spice Tan:** Paint lion's mane.
7. **AC Flesh:** Paint giraffe.
8. **Bambi:** Paint giraffe's spots and middle section of Ark (behind animals).
9. **Nightfall:** Paint top section of Ark.
10. **Dark Flesh:** Paint cat.
11. **Black:** Paint bird.
12. **Fleshtone:** Paint Noah's head and hands.
13. **Nightfall:** Shade Ark (bottom and middle sections) and elephant.
14. **Bambi:** Shade right side of Noah's beard and heart on Ark.
15. **Light Ivory:** Splatter entire piece lightly. Paint dots on giraffe's head. Very lightly line design on elephant.
16. **Dark Flesh:** Shade Noah's face and hands.
17. **Gypsy Rose:** Stipple cheeks on Noah, lion, giraffe and elephant. Paint dot hearts on stem in bird's mouth and on elephant's ear.
18. Black lining pen: Line/stitch everything, dot eyes, and line all details and letters.
19. Spray varnish.
20. Add buttons and jute bow if desired.
21. Add twisted wire or hooks to hang on one of the Country Welcome Signs or Birdhouse Stand.

NOAH'S ARK CLAY POT

Paint bottom of pot **Nightfall.** Paint Noah and animals following Noah's Ark Instructions. Lightly splatter **Light Ivory.** Line in black lining pen. Fill with "rag balls" or any other Country Stuff!

HINT:

To make rag balls quick and easy, use various sizes of styrofoam balls. Wrap with one inch torn strips of country print fabric.

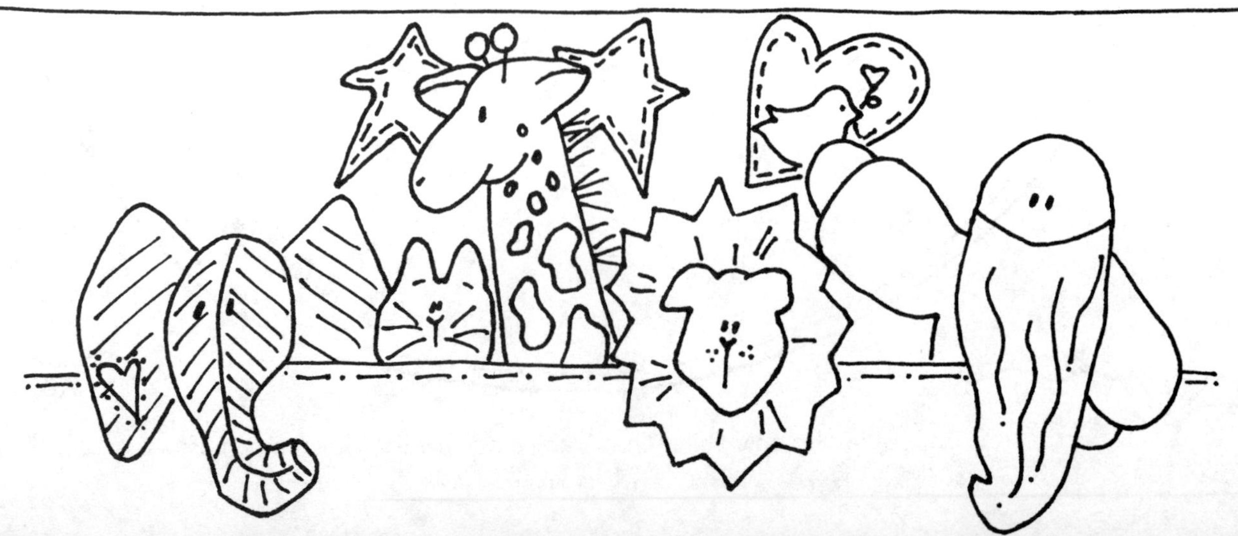

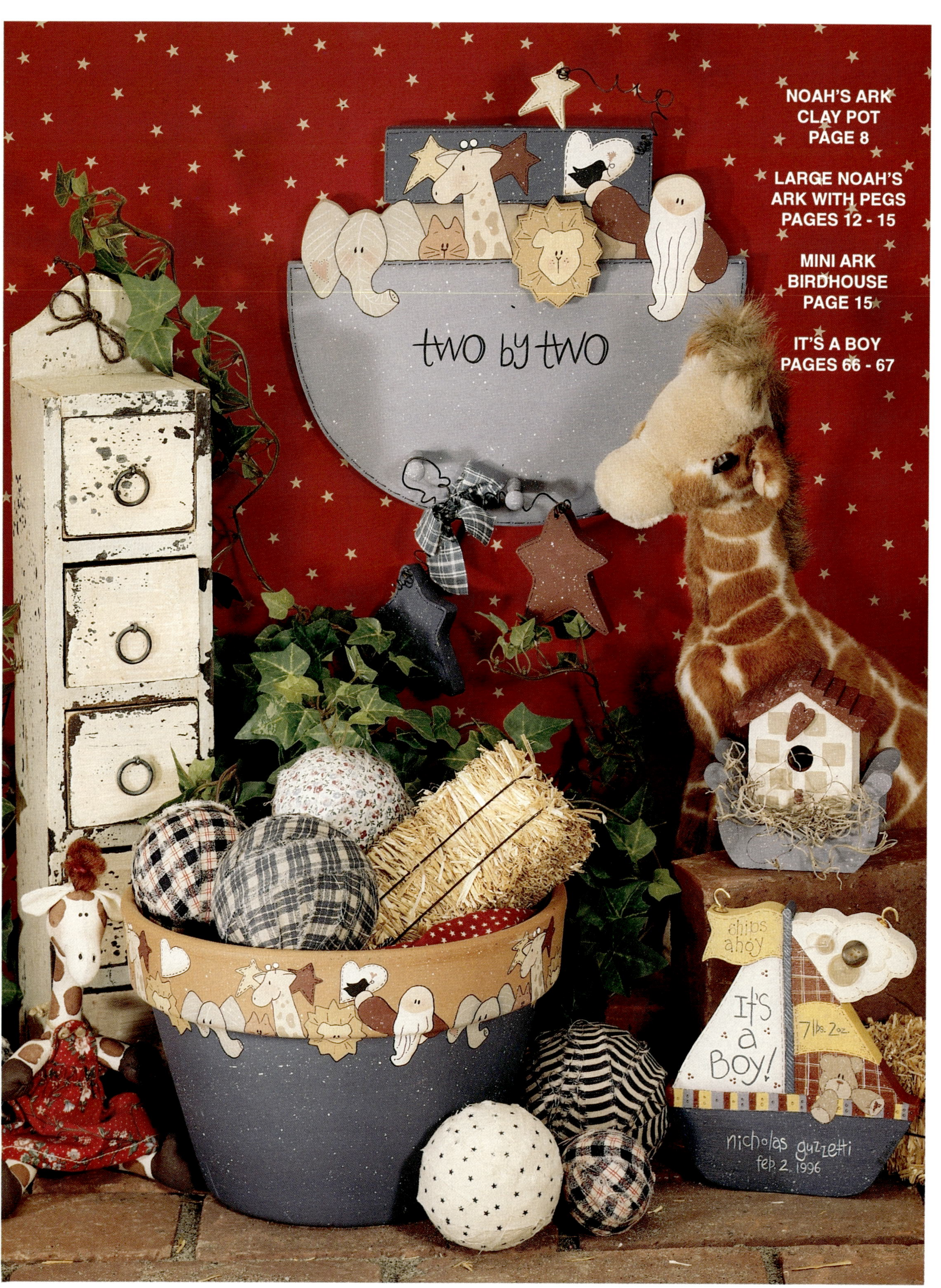
NOAH'S ARK
CLAY POT
PAGE 8

LARGE NOAH'S
ARK WITH PEGS
PAGES 12 - 15

MINI ARK
BIRDHOUSE
PAGE 15

IT'S A BOY
PAGES 66 - 67

two by two

chips ahoy

It's a Boy!

7 lbs. 2 oz.

nicholas guzzetti
feb. 2, 1996

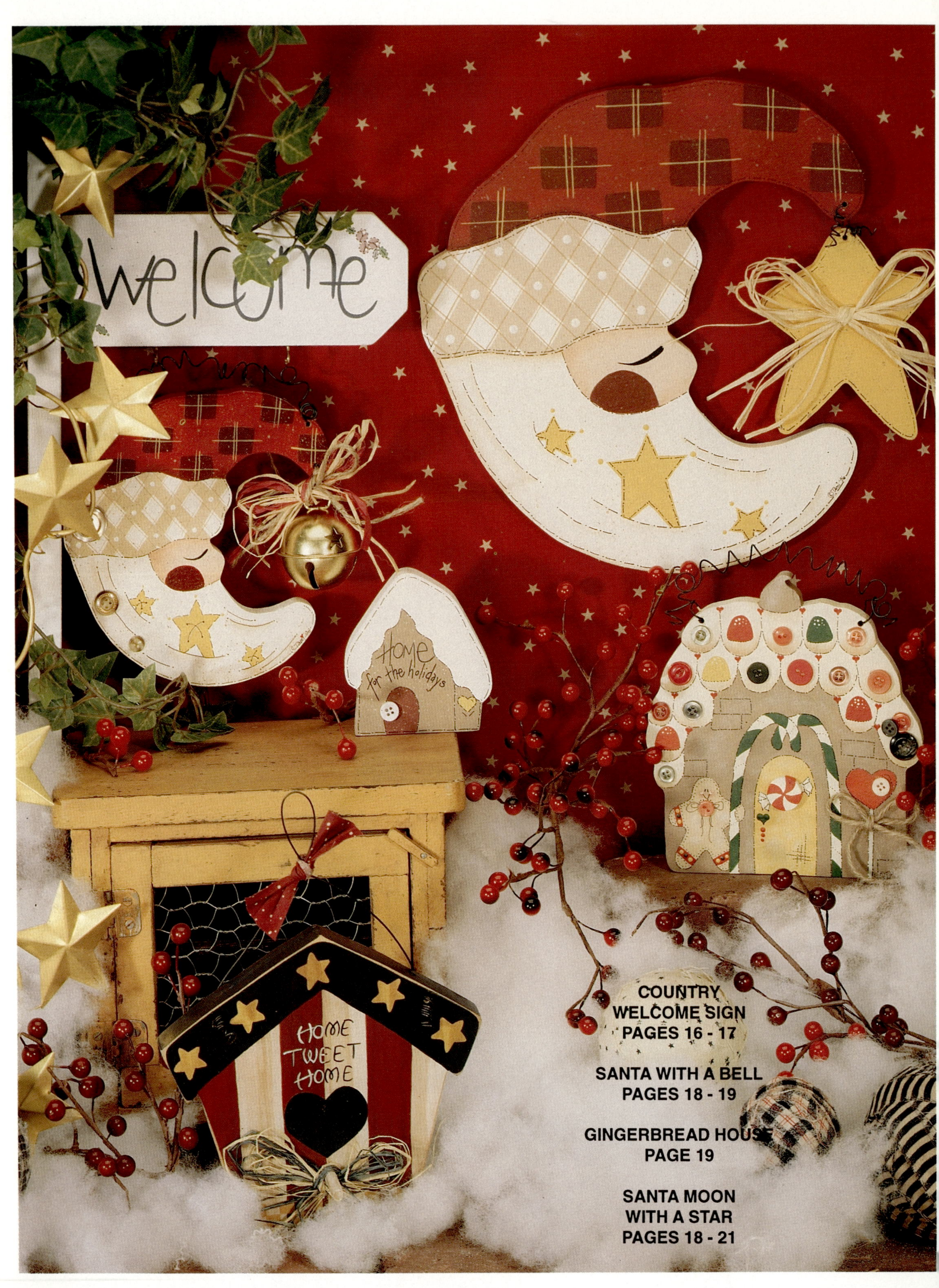
welcome
Home for the holidays
HOME TWEET HOME
COUNTRY
WELCOME SIGN
PAGES 16 - 17

SANTA WITH A BELL
PAGES 18 - 19

GINGERBREAD HOUSE
PAGE 19

SANTA MOON
WITH A STAR
PAGES 18 - 21

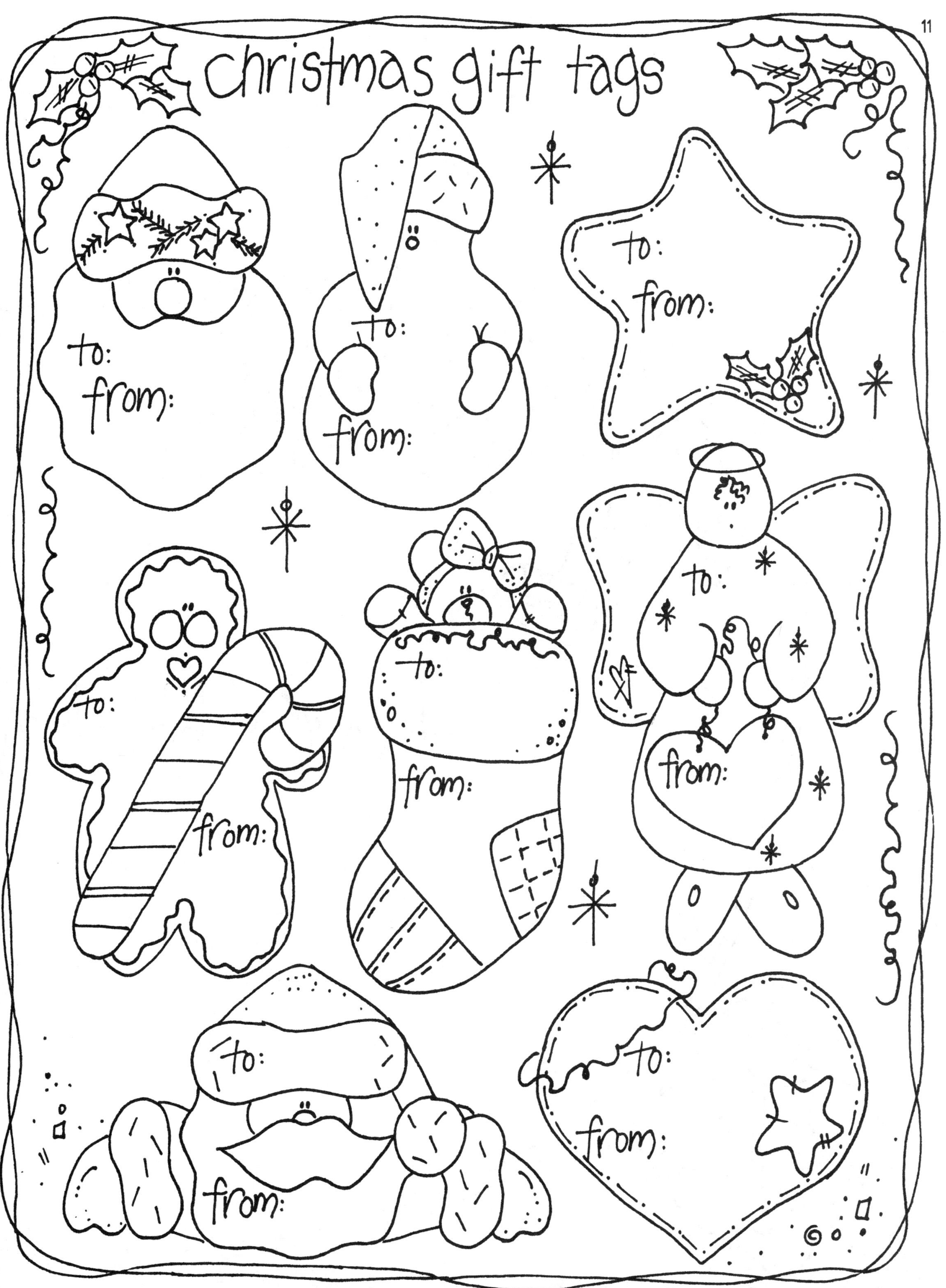

christmas gift tags
to:
from:
to:
from:
to:
from:
to:
from:
to:
from:
to:
from:
to:
from:
to:
from:

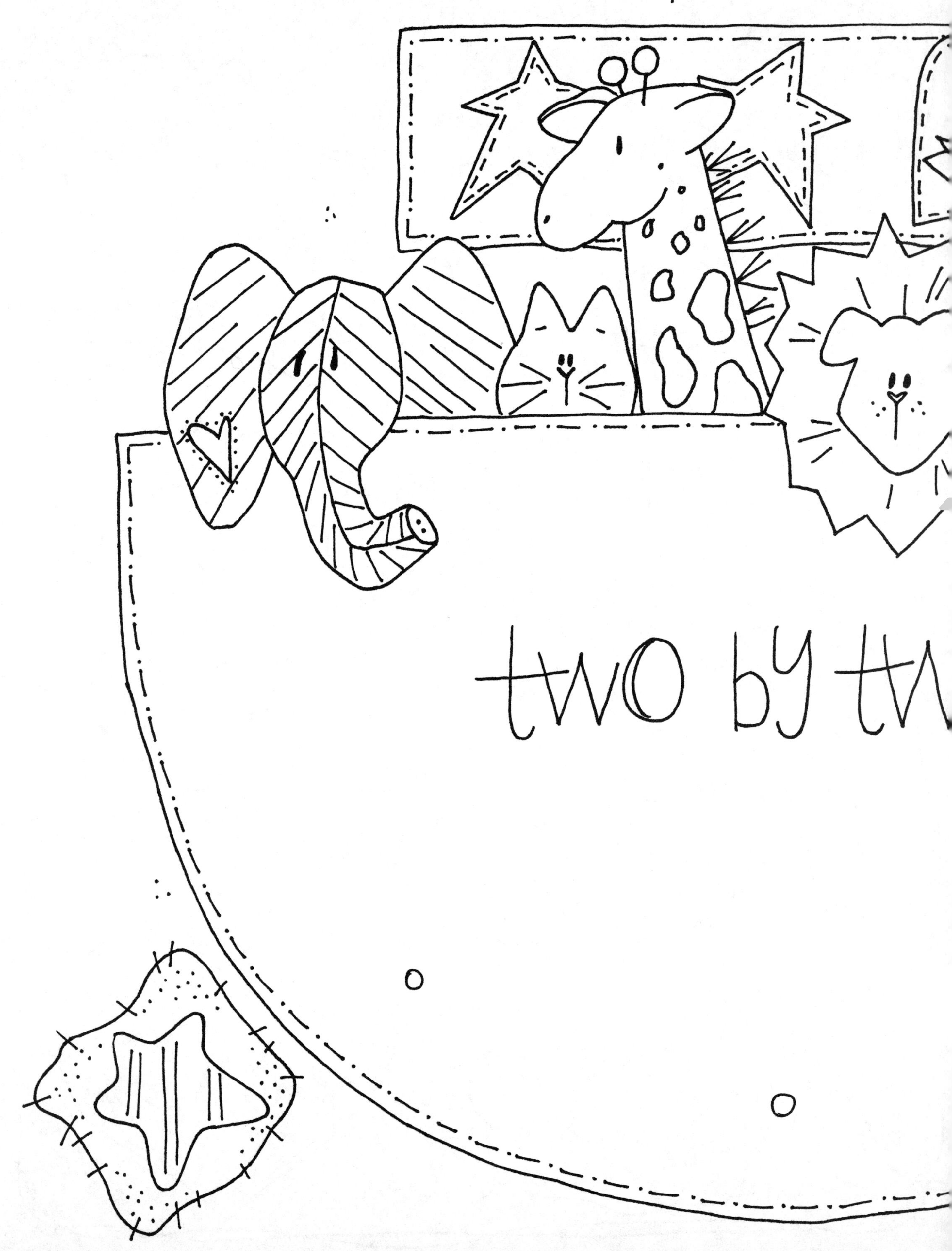

two by tw

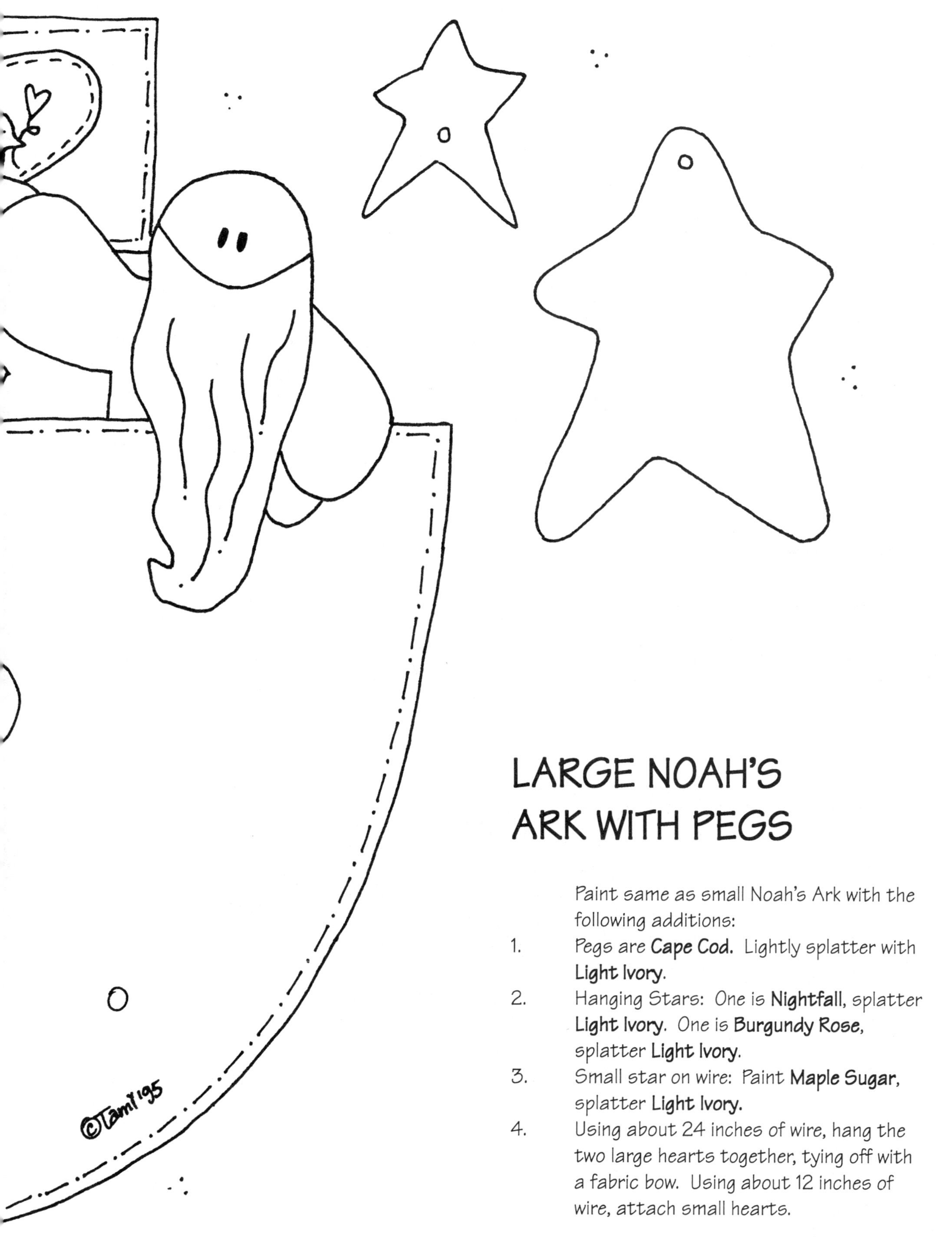

LARGE NOAH'S ARK WITH PEGS

Paint same as small Noah's Ark with the following additions:

1. Pegs are **Cape Cod**. Lightly splatter with **Light Ivory**.

2. Hanging Stars: One is **Nightfall**, splatter **Light Ivory**. One is **Burgundy Rose**, splatter **Light Ivory**.

3. Small star on wire: Paint **Maple Sugar**, splatter **Light Ivory**.

4. Using about 24 inches of wire, hang the two large hearts together, tying off with a fabric bow. Using about 12 inches of wire, attach small hearts.

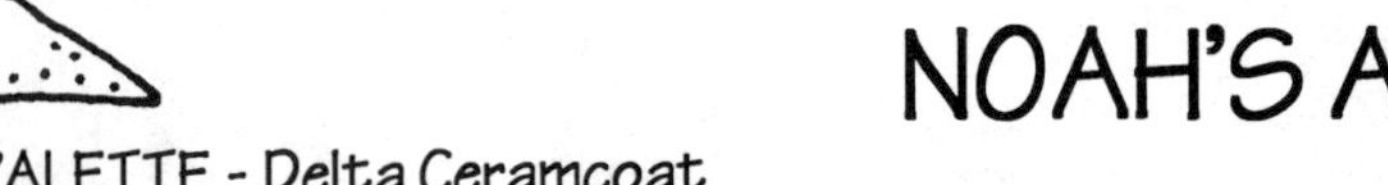

NOAH'S ARK

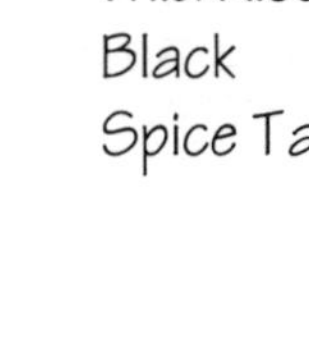

PALETTE - Delta Ceramcoat

Fleshtone	Cape Cod Blue	Light Ivory	Wild Rice
Tide Pool Blue	Bambi Brown	Burgundy Rose	Black
AC Flesh	Nightfall Blue	Maple Sugar	Spice Tan
Lichen Gray	Rose Cloud	Medium Flesh	

NOTE: Please refer to the fold-out page for patterns.

PAINTING NOAH AND HIS ARK

1. **Fleshtone:** Paint hands, face and foot.
2. **Light Ivory:** Paint beard and safety pin. *NOTE: Here's a tip for nice looking painting with colors that aren't so nice to use, like Light Ivory, White, yellows, even some reds and browns. The trick is to make sure each coat is a very even layer of color. It doesn't need to be good coverage as much as evenly painted on. To do this, try dipping one side of your paint brush in water, then your whole brush in paint. This seems to thin it enough, and give you a little more time to work with the paint before it dries out, giving even layers. Because the coats are even, you don't need as many of them! Also, be sure to let each coat dry completely before starting another layer of paint.
3. **Cape Cod Blue:** Paint Noah's clothes.
4. **AC Flesh:** Paint giraffes.
5. **Bambi Brown:** Paint giraffe's spots and middle of Ark (behind animals).
6. **Nightfall Blue:** Paint top of Ark.
7. **Maple Sugar:** Paint lions.
8. **Spice Tan:** Paint lion's mane.
9. **Lichen Gray:** Paint elephants.
10. **Rose Cloud:** Paint bows on female animals.
11. **Black:** Paint Noah's eyes.
12. **Burgundy Rose:** Paint Noah's nose, large heart, bottom of Ark, lion's noses and small heart on elephant. Shade cheeks.
13. **Tide Pool Blue:** Paint squares on Noah's clothes.
14. **Wild Rice:** Paint thick lines in beard.
15. Mix equal parts of **Wild Rice** and **Light Ivory** - Paint Noah's moustache.
16. **Light Ivory:** Dot where thick lines intersect.
17. **Bambi Brown:** Line the thin wavy lines in beard. Shade safety pin. Lightly shade elephants and giraffes. Shade bottom of moustache and beard.
18. **Nightfall Blue:** Shade Noah's clothes (under sleeve and beard, around Ark and animals).
19. **Rose Cloud:** Stipple cheeks on animals.
20. **Medium Flesh:** Shade hands, foot and face. Stipple on foot, top of head and hands.
21. **Wild Rice:** Paint ribbon on sleeve. Paint "Welcome Aboard" on Ark. (I like the No. 4 round brush for this).
22. **Light Ivory:** Line highlight in Noah's eyes. Dot giraffe's horns. Lightly line design on elephants.
23. Patch on Sleeve - Checks are **Nightfall Blue** and **Light Ivory**. Center is **Burgundy Rose**. Dots are **Light Ivory**.
24. Patch on Ark - Paint **Nightfall Blue**. Lines are **Light Ivory**.
25. Lining Pen or Black paint: Line/stitch everything.
26. **Light Ivory:** Splatter all pieces lightly.
27. Glue arm to body.

PAINTING NOAH AND HIS ARK (Continued)

28. Spray all pieces well, 2 or 3 coats, with finishing spray/varnish. If you have not used a pen and desire to put Noah outside as a front porch ornament, you should use a brush-on varnish that will protect him better than a spray. (You can spray your pieces, then use waterbased sealer if you'd like extra protection).

29. Glue on buttons. Tear fabric pieces into one inch strips. Wrap staff with main color, gluing every several turns or so to secure in place. Then wrap and glue the accent color. Cut the rest of the fabric strips into 22 inch lengths, hold together and tie into one big knot. Glue staff to arm, hand to staff, and knot under hand.

You did it! May you enjoy your Noah and may he "welcome aboard" your country friends... much longer than 40 days and 40 nights!

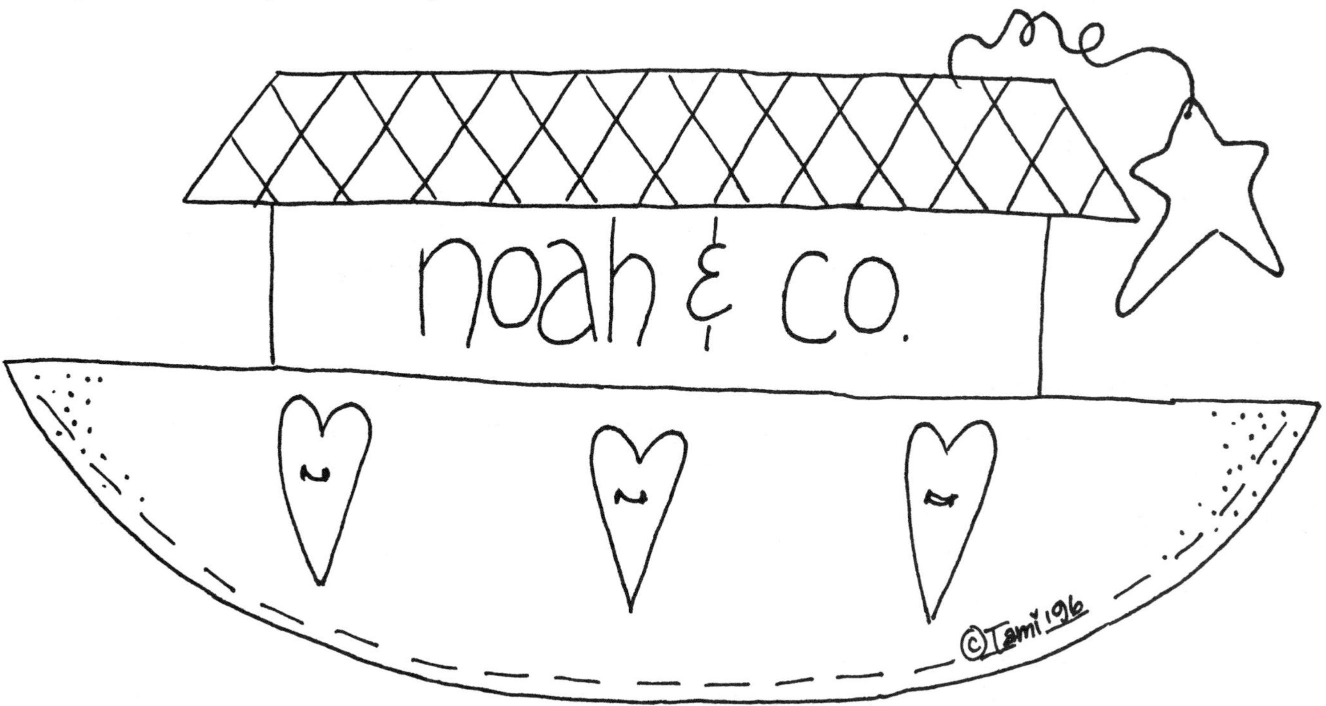

MINI ARK BIRDHOUSE

PALETTE - Delta Ceramcoat

Cape Cod　　　　　Queen Anne's Lace
Trail Tan　　　　　Burgundy Rose

SUPPLIES

Small Wooden Heart Button
Spanish Moss

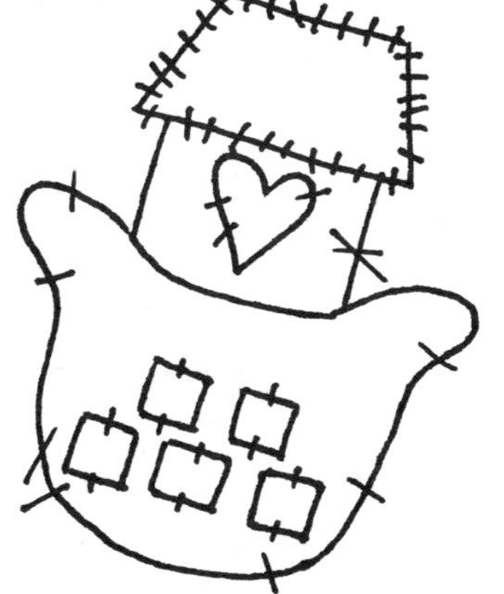

1. **Cape Cod:** Paint bottom of Ark.
2. **Queen Anne's Lace:** Paint birdhouse section of Ark.
3. **Trail Tan:** Paint checks on birdhouse.
4. **Burgundy Rose:** Paint roof, perch and heart button.
5. **Queen Anne's Lace:** - Splatter.
6. Spray varnish.
7. Glue on moss, heart and button.

COUNTRY WELCOME SIGN

No country lover should be without a Welcome Sign to greet their Country Guests! You can choose a flat sign or this sign with an "arm". With all the interchangeable designs you have, you can individualize your Country Welcome Sign to any holiday or occasion!

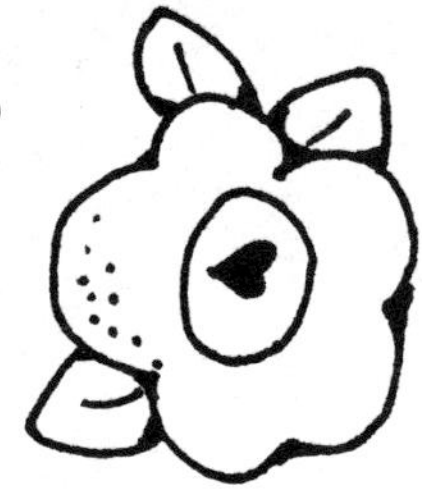

PALETTE - Delta Ceramcoat

White	Cape Cod	Sachet Pink
Green Sea	Nightfall	Cactus Green
Bouquet Pink		

SUPPLIES
Raffia

NOTE: Please refer to the fold-out page for painting patterns.

1. **Bouquet Pink:** Paint the hearts.
2. **White:** Paint the remaining pieces of the sign, the base piece with the "arm" and house. (Remember to paint both sides of each piece for both will show).
3. **Cape Cod:** Paint the roof on house. Lightly splatter all white pieces.
4. **Sachet Pink:** Highlight the top of the hearts. Paint the chimney on house.
5. **White:** Splatter the roof lightly.
6. **Nightfall:** Carefully paint the WELCOME letters on both sides of the "arm" of sign and ENTER WITH A HAPPY on both sides of the house. Dot ends of letters.
7. **Green Sea:** Line the vine.
8. **Bouquet Pink:** Paint the flowers.
9. **Green Sea** and **Cactus Green:** Using a stylus or the wooden end of a small brush, "dot and drag" the leaves, making some leaves the lighter green and some the darker. The color change is subtle but it helps to add dimension to use both colors.
10. **Bouquet Pink:** Shade bottom of chimney.
11. **Nightfall:** Lightly shade under roof line.
12. **Sachet Pink:** Paint the checks.
13. **Bouquet Pink:** Shade left side of checks.
14. **Cactus Green:** Paint comma strokes by heart on house.
15. **Green Sea:** Shade bottom of comma strokes.
16. **White:** Dot tips of flowers.
17. Black Lining Pen: Stitch around hearts, house, roof and chimney. Stitch around flowers and leaves.
18. Glue hearts to house and base of sign.
19. Spray with varnish.
20. Glue raffia bow to house.
21. Attach hooks and wire.

One of my painting students painted this Country Welcome Sign as a wedding gift with several holiday and general designs that the newlyweds could enjoy all year. It also makes subsequent gifts easy to do... just paint another interchangeable design for their Country Welcome Sign! Way to go, Joanne!

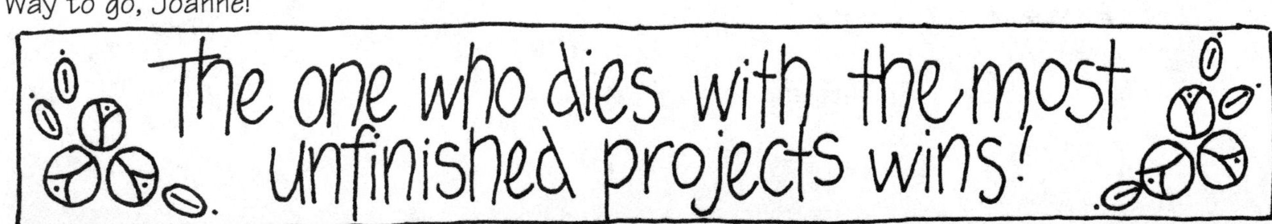

"arm" placement
COUNTRY WELCOME SIGN
base piece - tape together here
welcome
©Tami '95

SANTA WITH A BELL

PALETTE - Delta Ceramcoat

Light Ivory	Fleshtone	Butter Yellow
Bambi Brown	Maroon	Medium Flesh
AC Flesh	Tompte Red	Black

MISCELLANEOUS SUPPLIES

Buttons (Optional)	Natural/Red Raffia
Jute	Large Jingle Bell, 44 mm
Wire or Hooks	

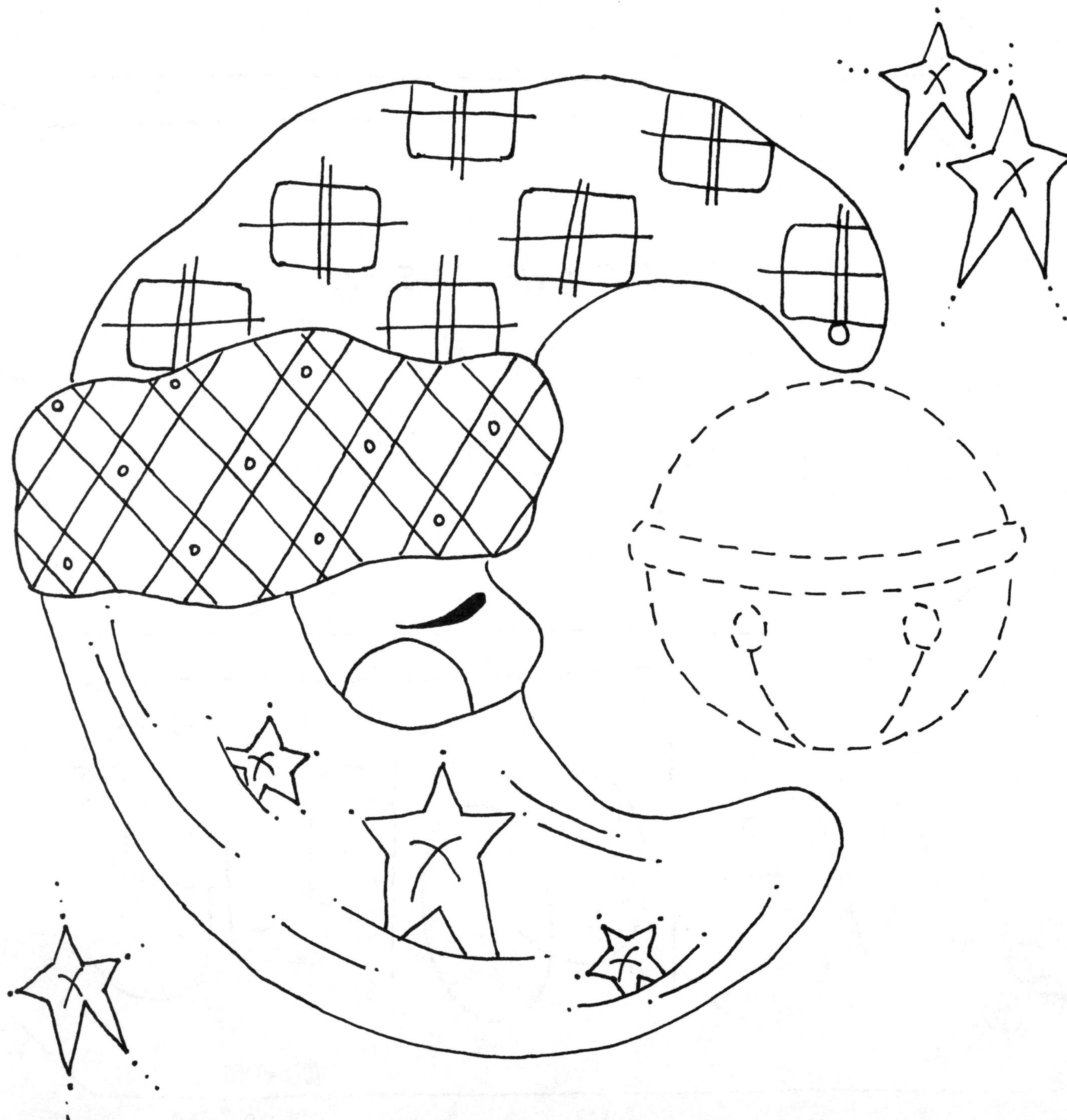

SANTA WITH A BELL Cont.

1. **Light Ivory:** Paint entire piece.
2. **Tompte Red:** Paint top of hat, leaving fur area **Light Ivory**.
3. **Fleshtone:** Paint face.
4. **Butter Yellow:** Paint stars in beard and dots at points of stars.
5. **Maroon:** Shade Santa's hat. Paint squares on hat.
6. Painting Details on Fur Area: Paint a **Light Ivory** dot where thick lines intersect.
7. **Butter Yellow:** Line through squares on hat.
8. **Medium Flesh:** Shade face.
9. **Maroon:** Paint cheeks.
10. **Bambi Brown:** Shade beard, bottom edge and under each line inside beard. Lightly splatter everything.
11. **Black:** Comma stroke eye.
12. Black Lining Pen: Line/stitch everything. Line eye. Line detail in stars.
13. Spray varnish.
14. Tie bell to tip of hat with jute. Tie raffia to jute and make a bow. Glue on buttons (optional).
15. Attach twisted wire or hooks to Santa to hang from one the Country Welcome Signs or Birdhouse Stand.

GINGERBREAD HOUSE

PALETTE - Delta Ceramcoat

Antique White	Bambi Brown	Butter Yellow
Christmas Green	Orange	AC Flesh
Tompte Red		

Note: Please refer to the fold-out page for the pattern.

MISCELLANEOUS SUPPLIES

Buttons
Wire or Hooks

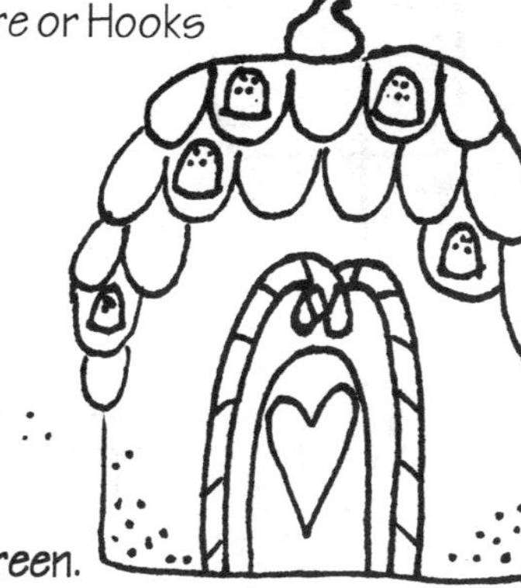

1. **Antique White:** Paint all pieces.
2. **Bambi Brown:** Paint house and chocolate drop candy chimney.
3. **Butter Yellow:** Paint door.
4. **Christmas Green:** Paint stripes on candy canes.
5. **Orange:** Paint heart lollipop.
6. Paint gumdrops **Butter Yellow**, **Tompte Red** and **Christmas Green**.
7. **AC Flesh:** Paint gingerbread boy.
8. **Bambi Brown:** Lightly shade scallops on roof and underneath chocolate drop candy.
9. **Antique White:** Paint lollipop stitch. Dot tops of gumdrops. Lightly stipple house, gingerbread boy, chocolate drop candy, candy canes and lollipop. Dot small hearts on ends of gingerbread boy's mouth. Paint the candy wrapper on the door.
10. **Tompte Red:** Stipple cheeks on gingerbread boy. Paint stripes on mint candy circle.
11. Finishing touches on Gingerbread Boy: Paint stripes on his hands and feet using **Santa Red** with **Christmas Green** and **Butter Yellow** dots.
12. **Christmas Green:** Paint a dot door knob.
13. **Tompte Red:** Paint three small dots under door knob, and paint dot hearts on roof.
14. Black Lining Pen: Line or dot/stitch everything.
15. Glue on buttons and jute bow.
16. Spray varnish.
17. Attach hooks or wire to hang from one of the Country Welcome Signs or Birdhouse Stand.

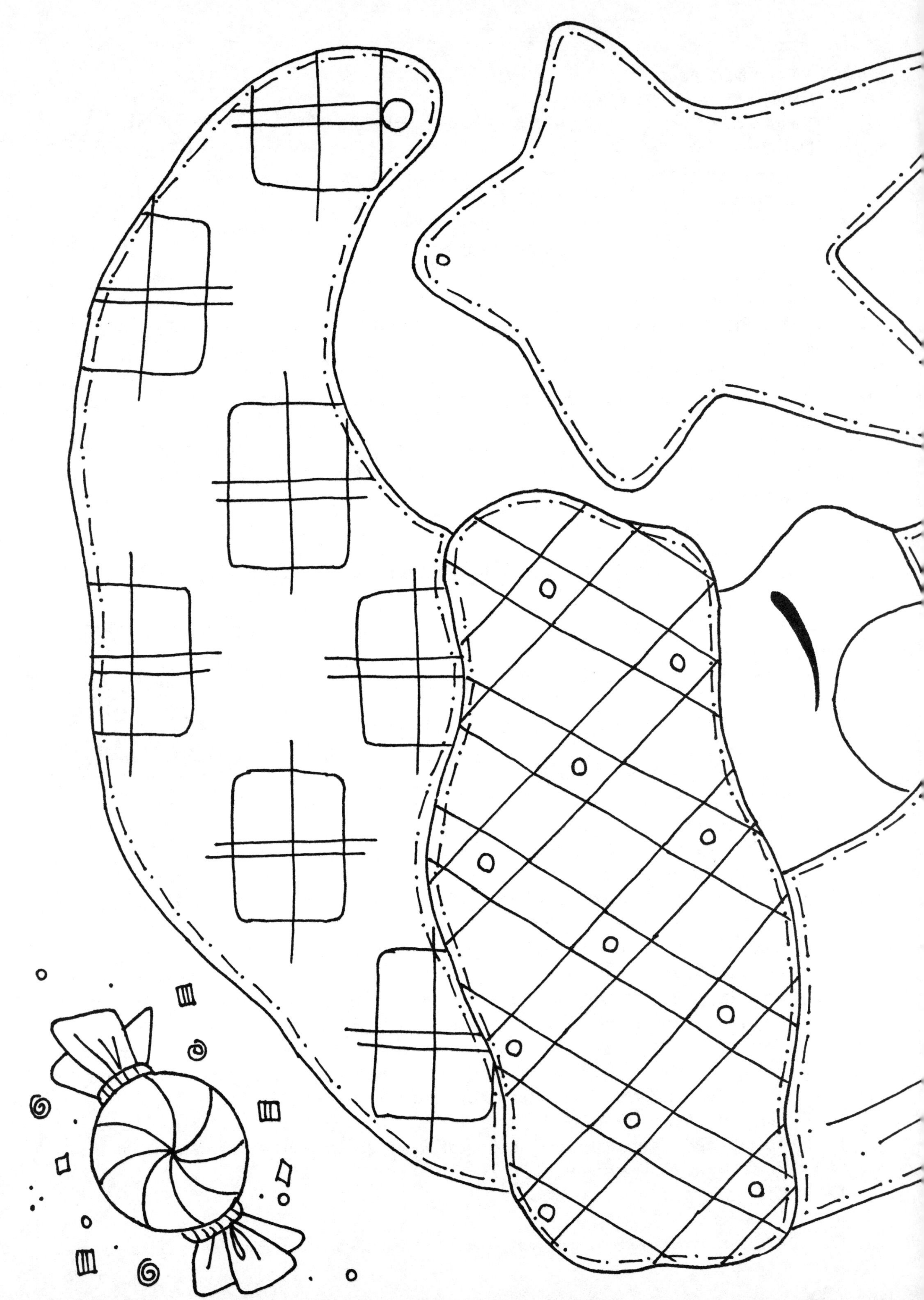

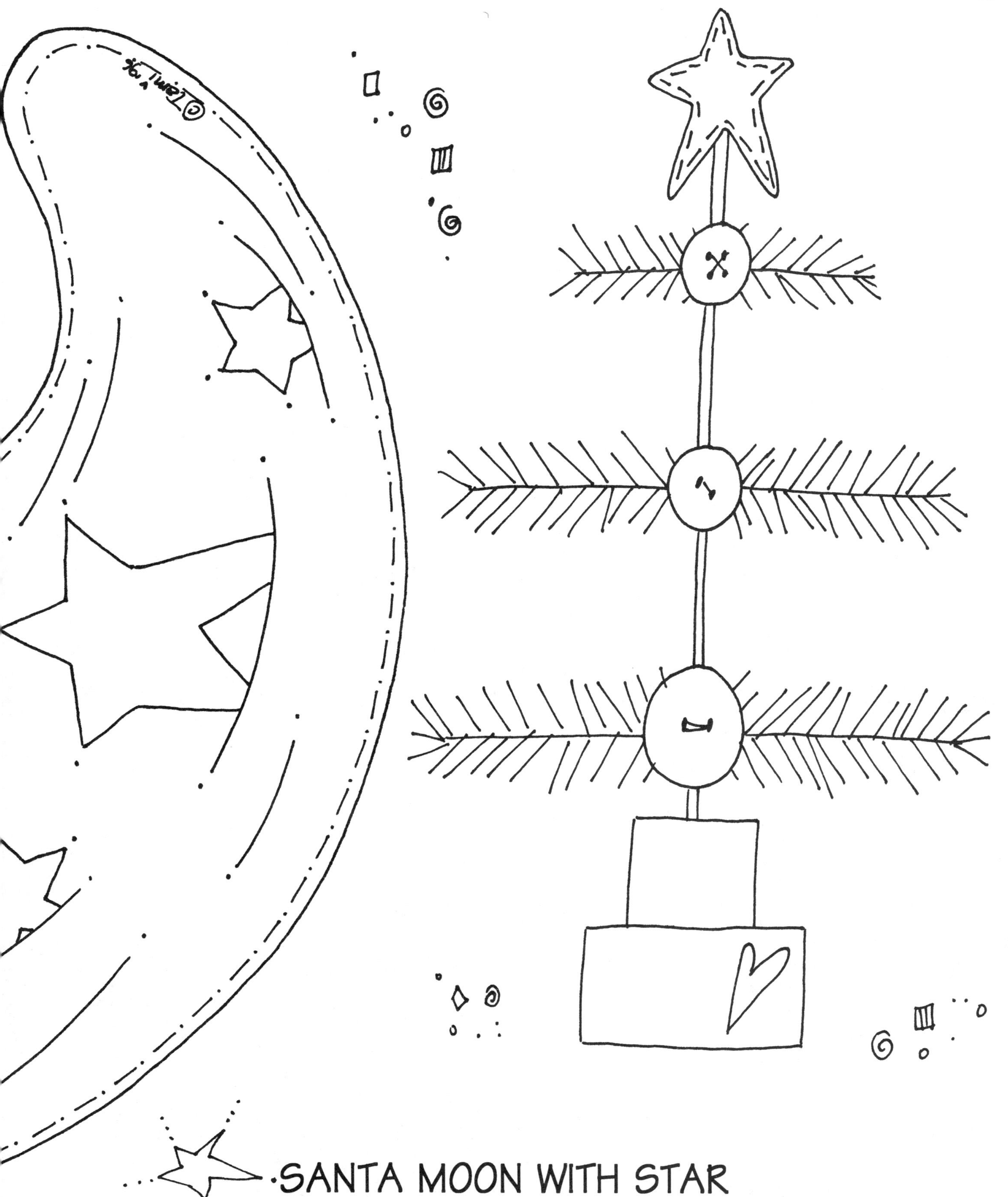

SANTA MOON WITH STAR

Paint according to instructions for Santa With Bell. Hanging star is **Butter Yellow**. Attach star to Santa Moon with twisted wire.

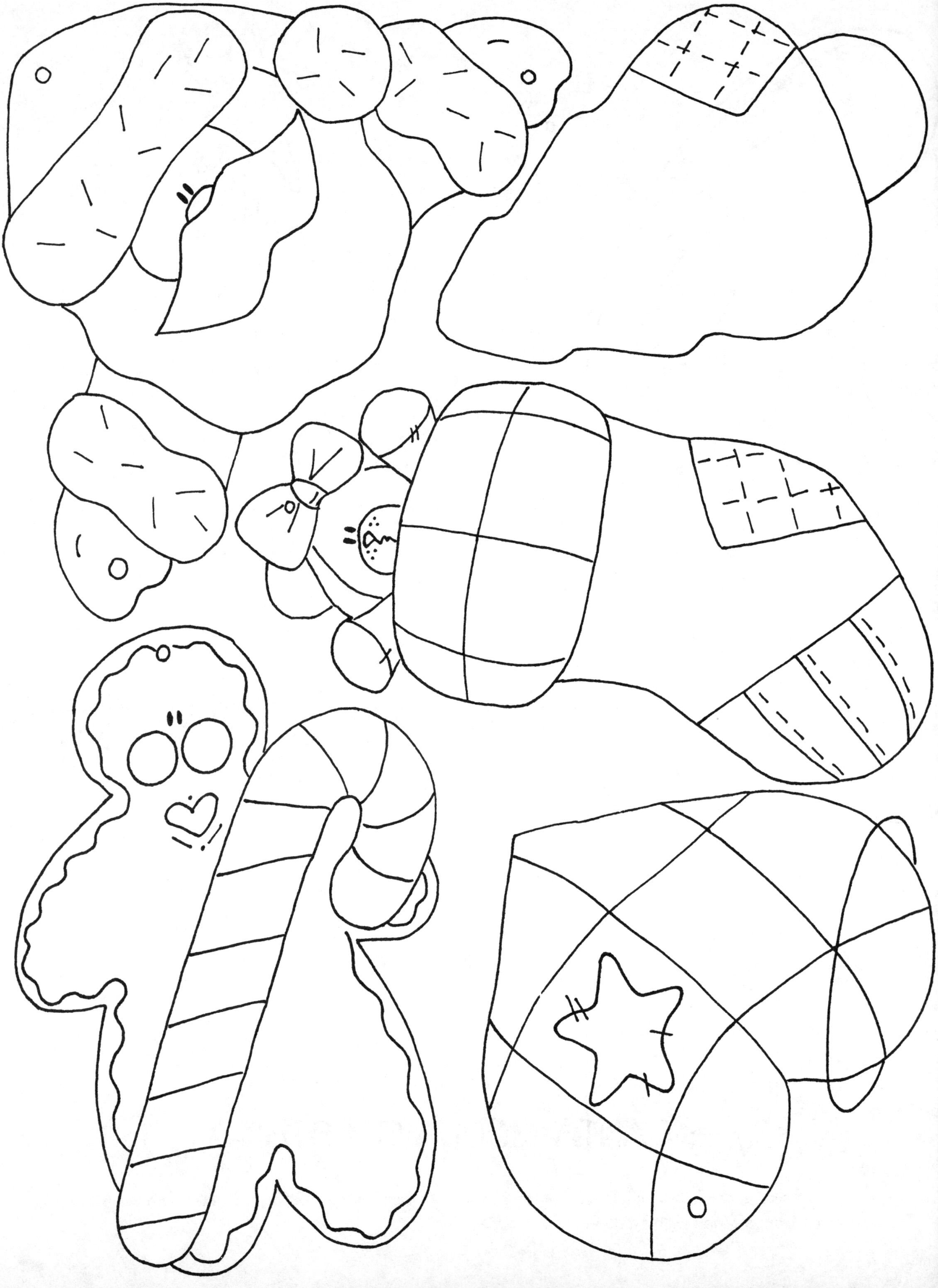

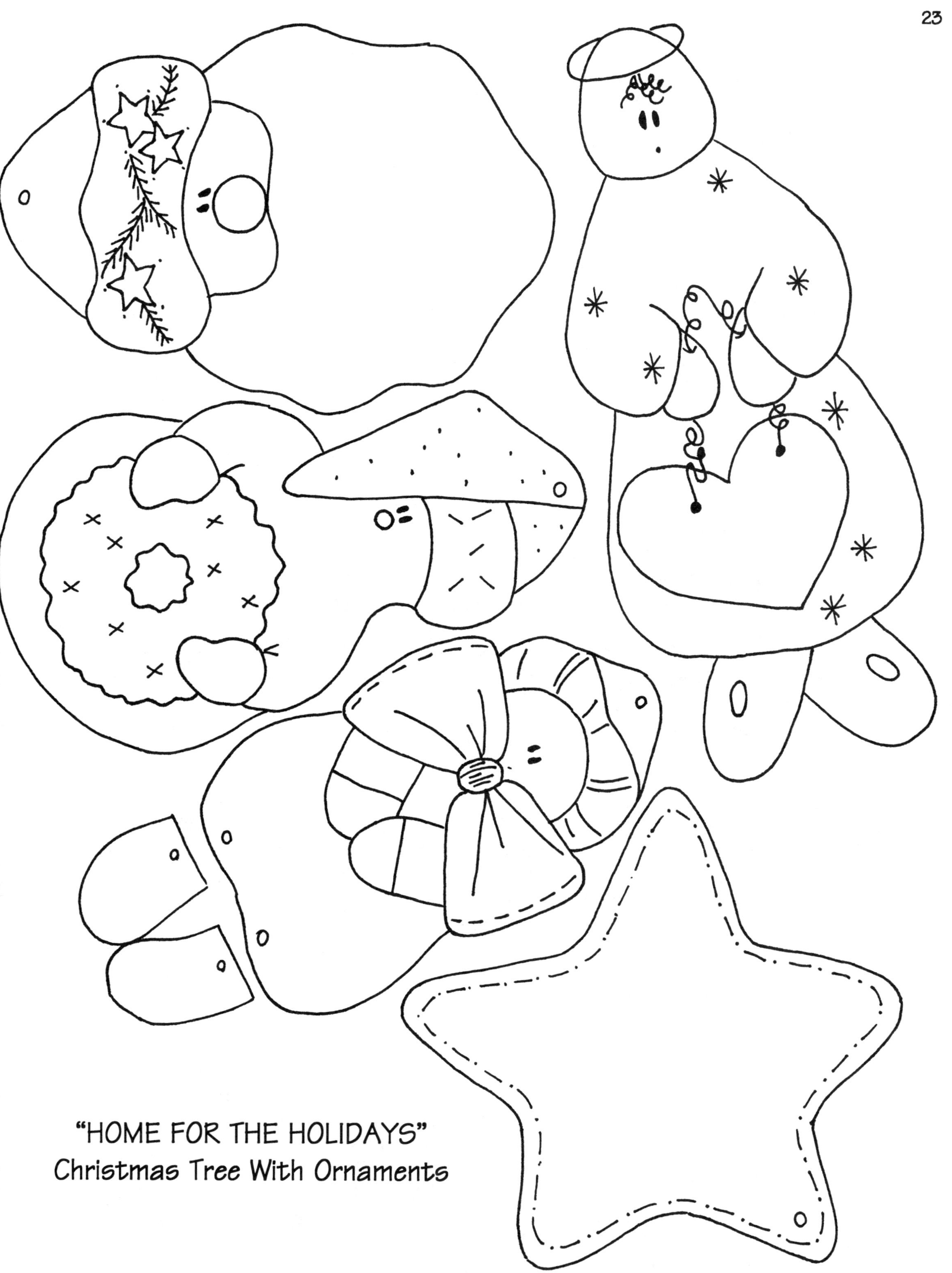

"HOME FOR THE HOLIDAYS"
Christmas Tree With Ornaments

CHRISTMAS BUNNY WITH BABIES

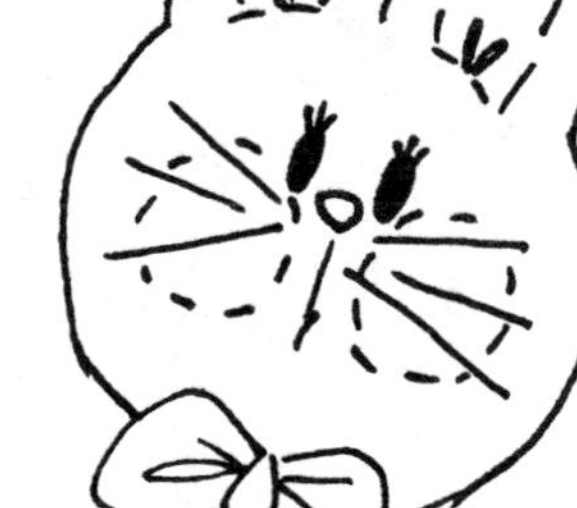

PALETTE - Delta Ceramcoat

Light Ivory	Sunbright Yellow	Black	AC Flesh
Christmas Green	Burgundy Rose	Bambi Brown	White
Sachet Pink	Candy Bar Brown	Deep River Green	

MISCELLANEOUS SUPPLIES

Six Inch Battenburg Lace Doily, Tea Dyed   1/8 Inch Ribbon, Red and Green

Three One Inch Wooden Hearts   Spanish Moss

Christmas Fabric: Knots at Feet 1" x 4"

           Fabric Drape 4-1/2" x 14"

           Bow 1" x 14"

1. **AC Flesh:** Paint big bunny's face, ears, hands, legs and entire baby bunny pieces.
2. **Light Ivory:** Paint fur on dress, fur on hat, snow on ground, the three heart pieces and the present.
3. **Burgundy Rose:** Paint all holly berries, dress and hat.
4. **Christmas Green:** Paint all holly leaves.
5. **Black:** Paint eyes.
6. **Sachet Pink:** Stipple cheeks and middle of ears.
7. **Gypsy Rose:** Paint noses and small heart on cheek. Stipple a deeper shade on bottom of ears and cheeks.
8. **White:** To make bunnies soft looking, stipple "bunny fur" on big bunny's face, ears, hands, feet and on baby bunnies. Dot highlight on cheeks. Stroke highlight on cheeks and dots in eyes.
9. **Bambi Brown:** Shade on the fur of dress and hat. Shade"C" strokes here and there on fur. Very lightly shade snow, outside edges of the three heart pieces, and the present's bow. Do three dot design on snow. Shade baby bunnie's faces, ears, hands and feet.
10. **Candy Bar Brown:** Shade dress on all outside edges and above fur on hat and dress. Shade bottoms of all holly berries.
11. **Deep River Green:** Shade bottom of all holly leaves. Shade under bow on present.
12. **Christmas Green:** Using end of small brush or toothpick, do three-dot pattern on dress. Paint designs on the three heart pieces.
13. **Black:** Lightly splatter the three heart pieces.
14. **Sunbright Yellow:** Very lightly stipple here and there on dress and hat. Stroke highlight on all holly berries. Line plaid lines on all holly leaves.
15. **Black Lining Pen:** Line everything.
16. Spray varnish.
17. Paint design on doily by laying doily over design, tracing design carefully and painting following instructions for holly berries and leaves at bunny's feet. Cut doily as illustrated. Glue to neck, tucking cut edges under and overlapping in the back. Glue fabric bow to hat, knots to feet and ribbon bows to babies. Glue heart pieces to dress, babies and present to dress. Tuck Spanish Moss around babies and present.

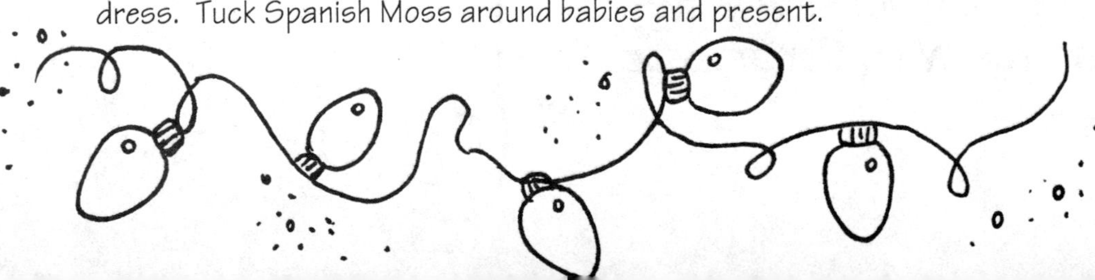

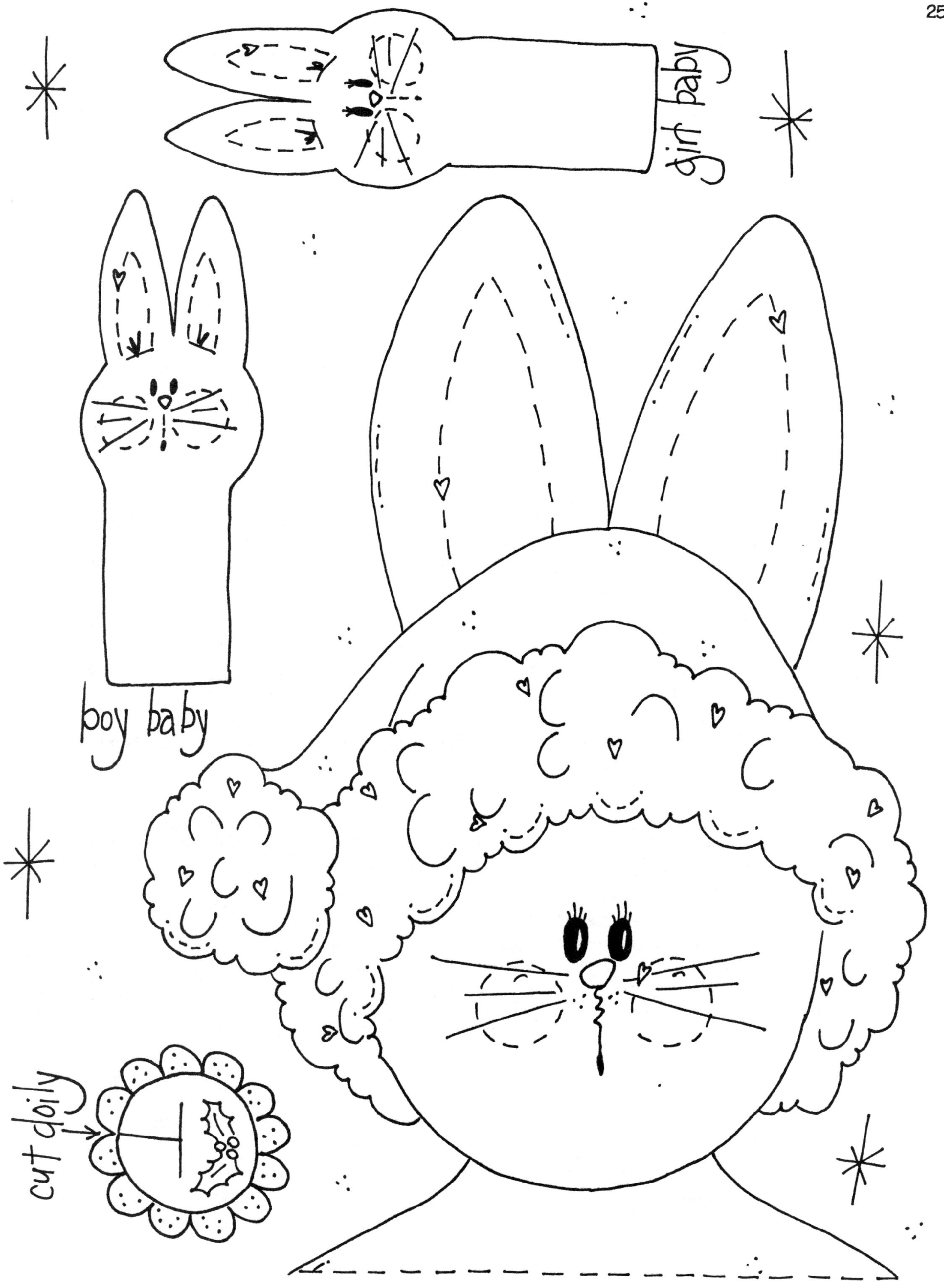
girl baby
boy baby
cut doily

"HOME FOR THE HOLIDAYS"
Christmas Tree With Ornaments

PALETTE - Delta Ceramcoat

Butter Yellow	White	Fleshtone	Burgundy Rose
Bambi Brown	Gypsy Rose	Light Ivory	Christmas Green
Deep River Green			

MISCELLANEOUS SUPPLIES

Two Screw Hole Buttons for 3/4 Inch Holes	Wire, 14 Inches
Paper Crimp Hair, White	Star Garland, Gold
Buttons (optional)	Jute, Approximately Seven Yards
Three Jingle Bells	Natural Raffia
Lining Pens, Black and Green	Fabric Scraps or 1/8 Yard Coordinating Colors

1. **SNOWMAN**
   Paint front and back **Light Ivory**. Top of hat and mittens are **Burgundy Rose**. Paint wreath **Christmas Green**. Dot nose and stipple cheeks **Gypsy Rose**. Bottom of hat is **Bambi Brown**. Stipple lightly here and there in **White**. Line eyes and details using black lining pen. Spray varnish. Glue jingle bell to bottom of hat. Tear strip of fabric 1" x 10", make bow, glue to bottom of wreath.

2. **HEART**
   Paint front and back **Light Ivory**. Paint every other check **Burgundy Rose**. Paint star **Butter Yellow**. Lightly splatter **White**. Line stitches using black lining pen. Spray varnish. Glue about six inches of star garland around one side of heart for a halo.

3. **ANGEL**
   Paint front and back **Light Ivory**. Hair is **Burgundy Rose**. Paint face and hands **Fleshtone**. Paint shoes **Bambi Brown**. Stipple cheeks **Gypsy Rose**. Stipple heart **Light Ivory**. Line eyes and details using black lining pen. Spray varnish. Glue button to front of dress. Tear fabric for wings in a six inch square. Fold fabric back and forth like a fan. Tie in center with another small strip of fabric. With right sides of fabric forward, glue wings to back of angel. Glue about three inches of star garland around forehead for a halo.

4. **CRIMP BEARD SANTA**
   Paint entire front and back **Light Ivory**. Face is **Fleshtone**. Stars are **Butter Yellow**. Top of hat is **Burgundy Rose**. Stipple cheeks and paint nose **Gypsy Rose**. Line greenery on hat using green lining pen. Line eyes and the rest of the details with black lining pen. Spray varnish. Glue paper-crimp hair to beard areas. (I take a small handful of the hair, gently brush it with my fingers so it all goes the same direction. I put glue on the painted beard, then place the hair on the beard. You can fill in an empty spot with several single strands if needed. Trim bottom of hair so it is even with edge of wood).

5. **GINGERBREAD BOY**
   Paint entire candy cane **Light Ivory**. Paint gingerbread boy and back **Bambi Brown**. Paint every other stripe on candy cane **Burgundy Rose**. Paint two screw hole buttons **Gypsy Rose**. Heart is **Butter Yellow**. Paint thin wavy line **Light Ivory**. Very lightly stipple center of candy cane and here and there on gingerbread boy in **White**. Line eyes and other details with black lining pen. Spray varnish. Glue screw hole buttons to face for cheeks. Glue on other buttons.

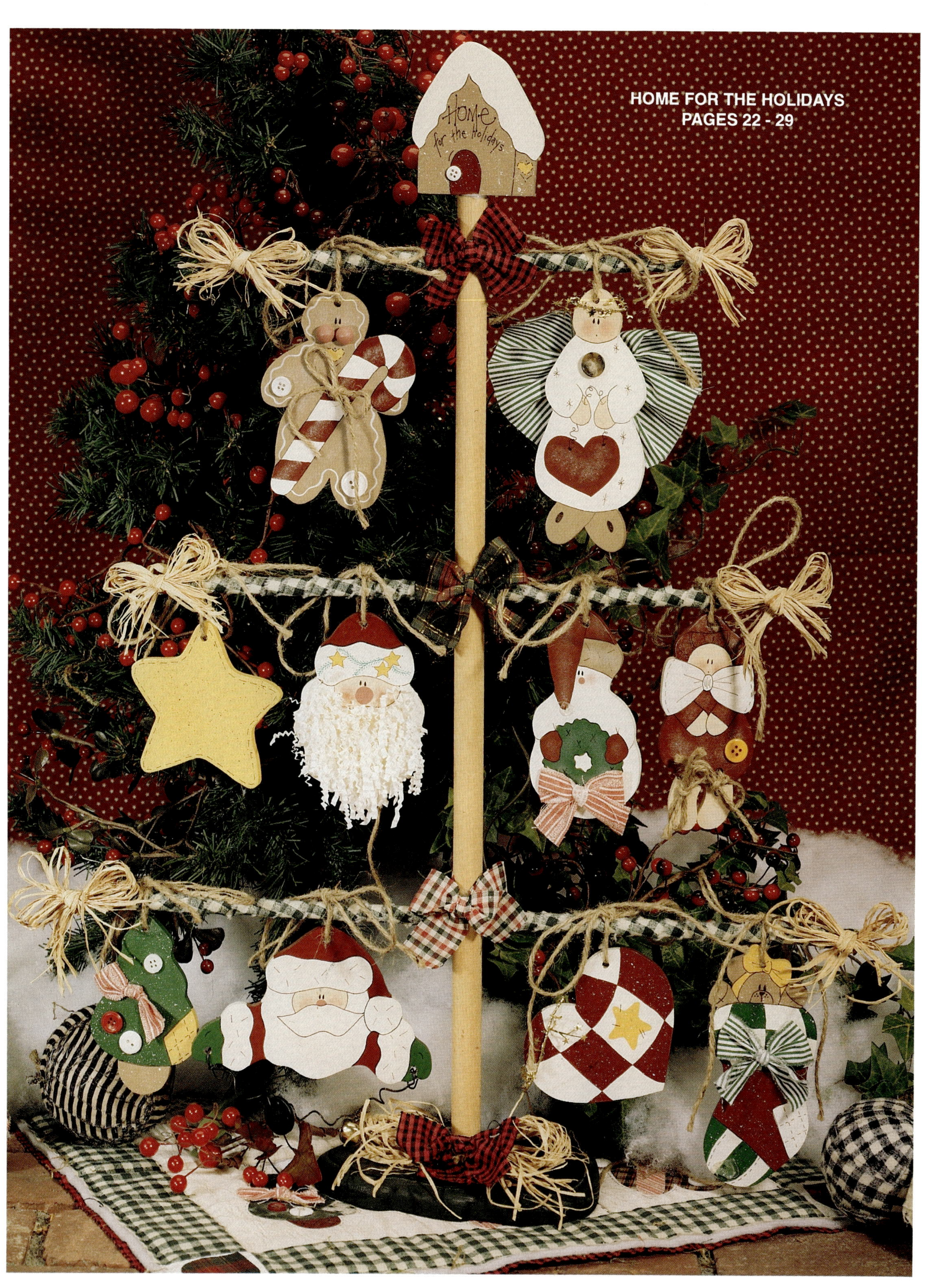

Home
for the Holidays

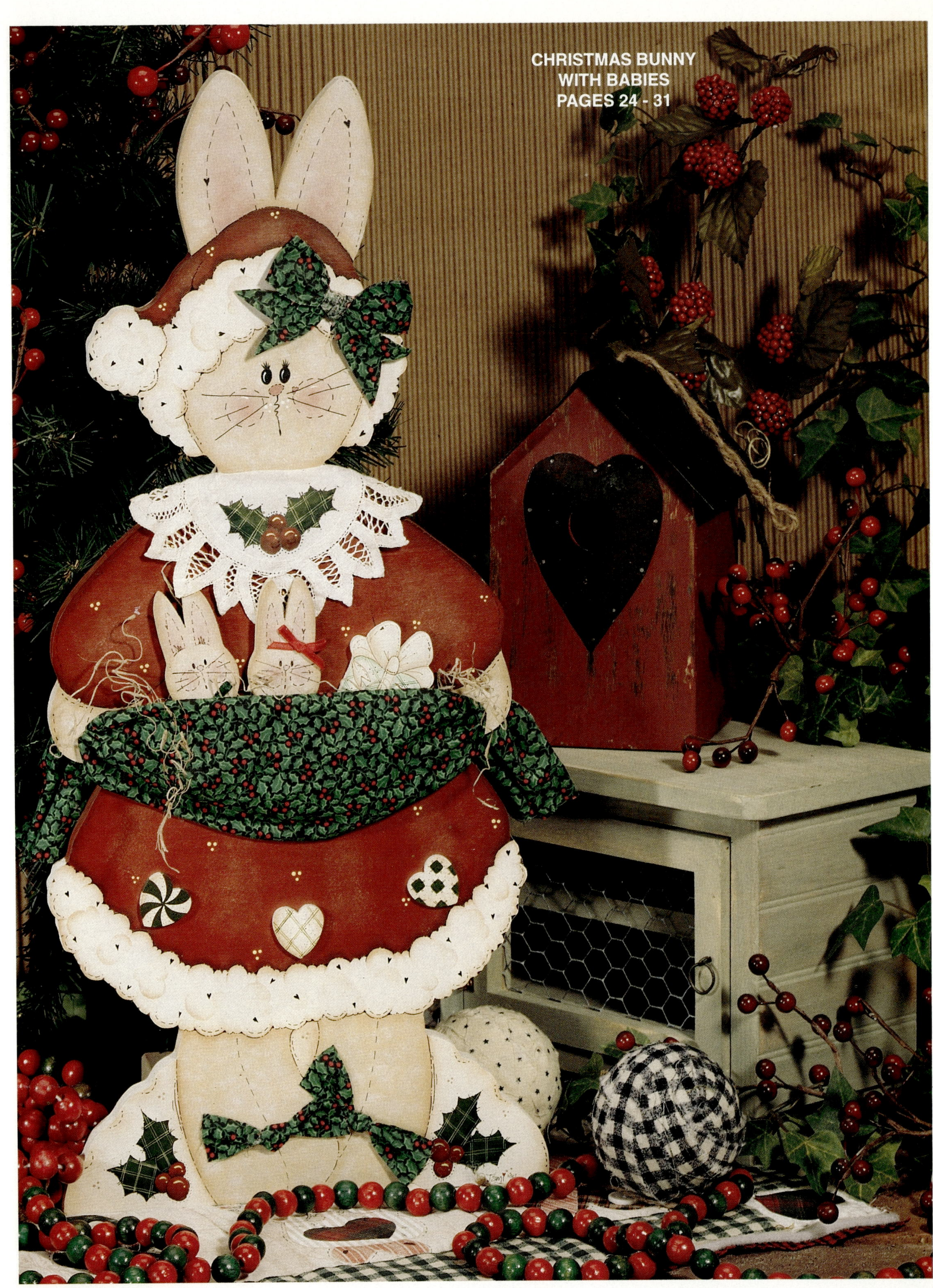
CHRISTMAS BUNNY
WITH BABIES
PAGES 24 - 31

HOME FOR THE HOLIDAYS Cont.

6. STAR

Paint front and back **Butter Yellow.** Lightly splatter **Burgundy Rose.** Using black lining pen, stitch around star. Spray varnish.

7. TREE

Paint patch **Butter Yellow.** The tree and back are **Christmas Green.** Paint trunk **Bambi Brown.** Splatter **Light Ivory.** Line in details with black lining pen. Spray varnish. Glue on buttons and a knot of fabric, 3/4" x 5".

8. STOCKING

Paint squares on top of stocking **Christmas Green** and **Light Ivory.** Stocking and back are **Burgundy Rose.** Heel patch is **Light Ivory.** Paint toe stripes **Christmas Green** and **Light Ivory.** Teddy bear is **Bambi Brown.** Paint bow on bear **Butter Yellow.** Splatter lightly with **White.** Line details with black lining pen. Spray varnish. Glue jingle bell to toe and jute bow on top of stocking.

9. SANTA WITH WIRE

Paint entire front and back **Light Ivory.** Paint face **Fleshtone.** Hat and sleeve are **Burgundy Rose.** Gloves are **Christmas Green.** Paint nose and stipple cheeks **Gypsy Rose.** Line in eyes and details with black lining pen. Spray varnish. Thread jingle bell and large button onto wire. Wrap ends through Santa's hands, twisting and curling wire as you go.

10. DOLL

Paint hands, feet and legs **Fleshtone.** Paint bow **Light Ivory.** Paint dress, hat and back in **Burgundy Rose.** Stipple cheeks **Gypsy Rose.** Stipple lightly here and there on the dress and hat in **White.** Using black lining pen, line eyes and details. Spray varnish. Using about 10 inches of jute, tie leg to body and make a bow. Repeat for other leg.

FINISHING ORNAMENTS

Tie approximately 24 inches of jute to top of each ornament. Leave a loop large enough to slide onto the tree then make a big bow. Hang your ornaments on a wooden tree or your own Country Christmas Tree!

TREE TOPPER

Paint house **Bambi Brown.** Paint snow **Light Ivory.** The heart is **Butter Yellow.** Paint door **Burgundy Rose.** Splatter **White.** Line the details using black lining pen. Spray varnish. Glue on button.

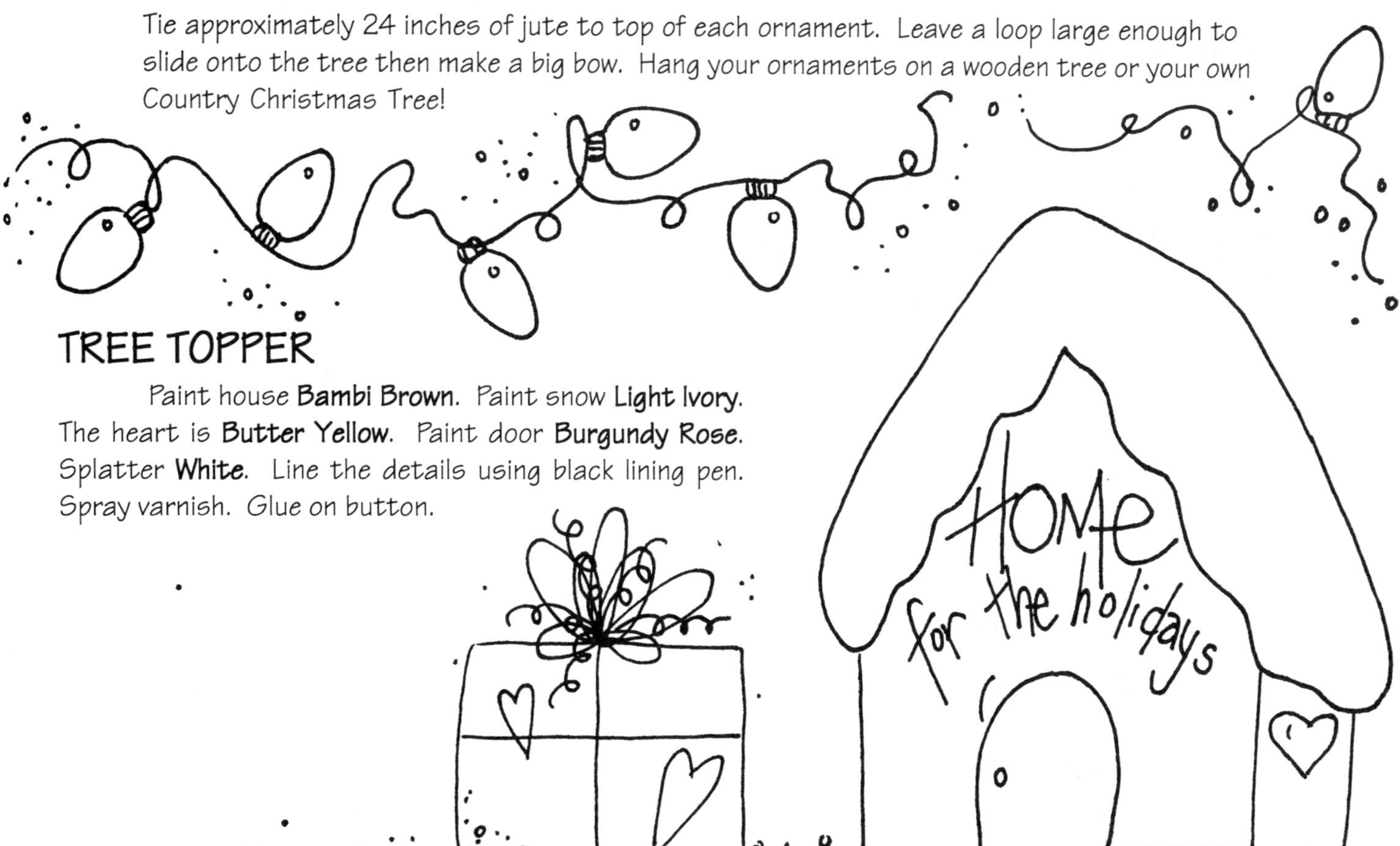

CHRISTMAS BUNNY WITH BABIES

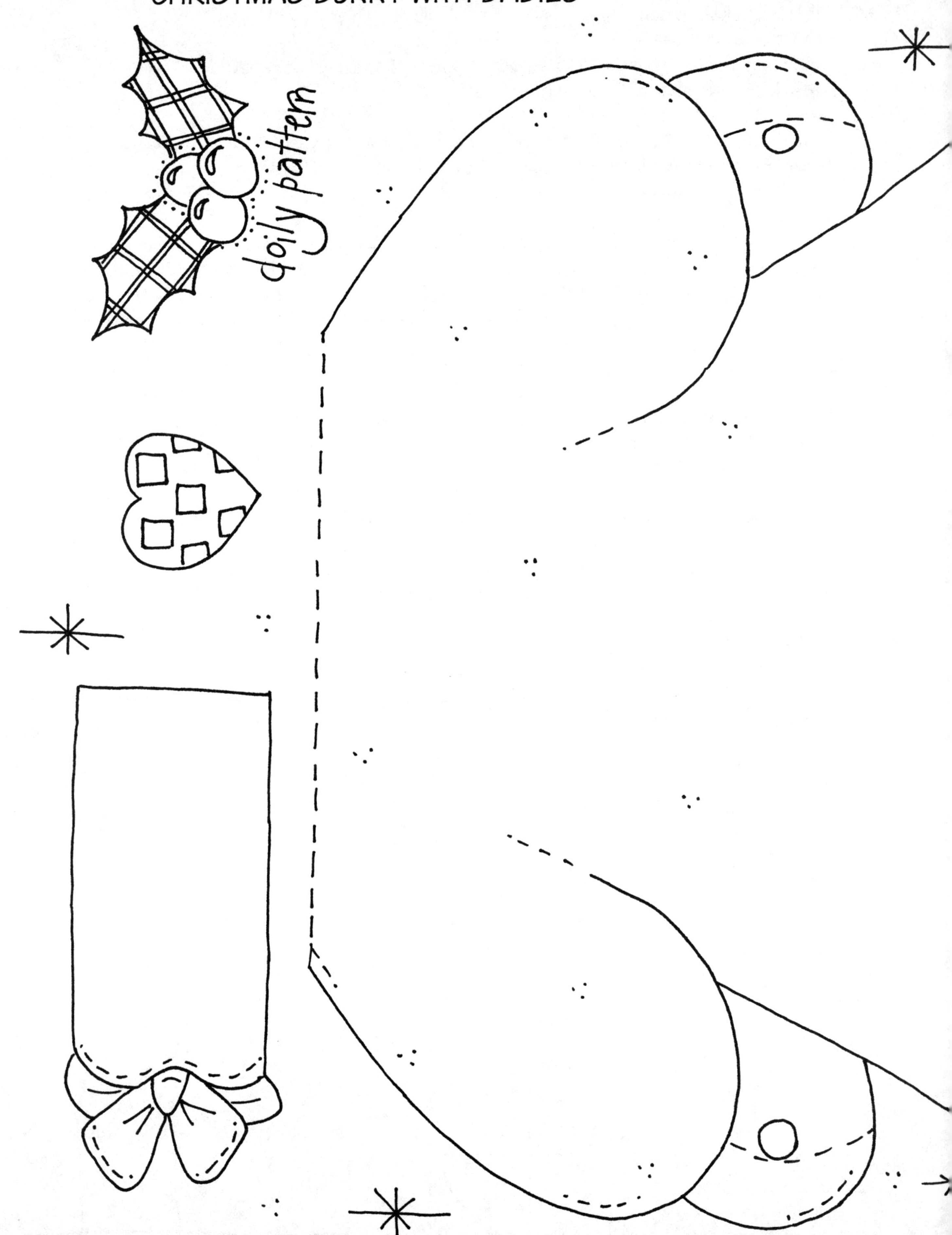

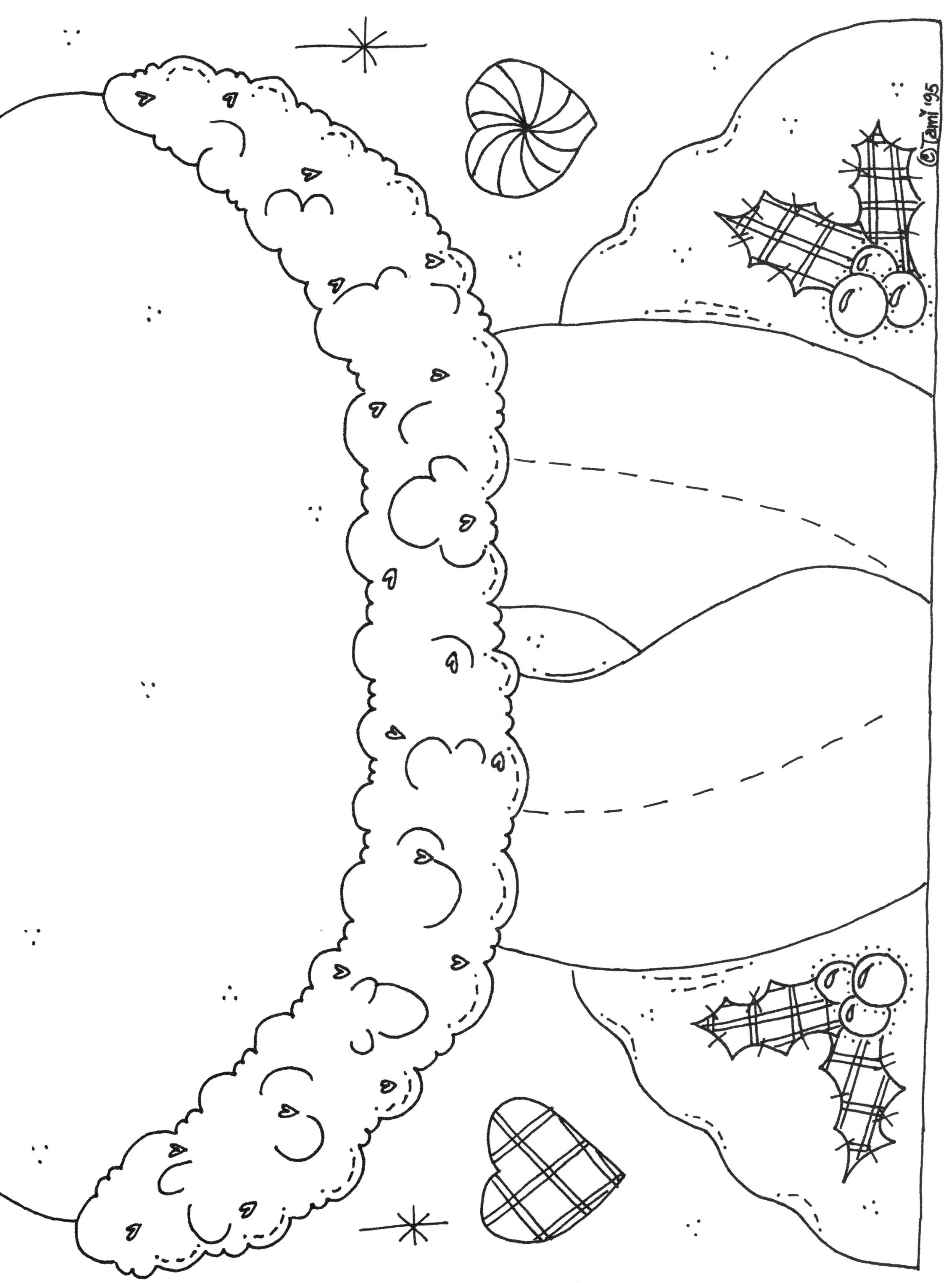

THANKSGIVING TREE

PALETTE - Delta Ceramcoat

Caucasian Flesh	Bambi Brown	Nightfall	Light Ivory
Wedgewood Green	Gypsy Rose	Dusty Mauve	Fleshtone

MISCELLANEOUS SUPPLIES

Natural Raffia	Buttons (Optional)	Jute	Wire

1. **PUMPKIN**
   The pumpkin is painted **Caucasian Flesh**. Stem is **Bambi Brown**. Paint leaves **Wedgewood Green**. The heart is **Light Ivory**. Using a black lining pen, line/stitch everything. Glue on buttons.

2. **TURKEY**
   Paint entire piece **Light Ivory**. Splatter lightly with **Bambi Brown**. Paint front row of feathers **Nightfall**. The beak and back row of feathers is **Caucasian Flesh**. Paint cheeks **Gypsy Rose**. The waddle is **Dusty Mauve**. Line eyes and stitch detail with a black lining pen. Glue on buttons and jute bow.

3. **PILGRIM GIRL**
   Paint entire piece **Light Ivory**. Splatter lightly with **Bambi Brown**. Paint face and hands **Fleshtone**. Dress and hat are **Nightfall**. With **Bambi Brown**, paint the basket, hair on head and line the braids. Stipple cheeks **Gypsy Rose** and line ribbons on braids. Paint the pumpkin in **Caucasian Flesh**. Leaves are **Wedgewood Green**. With black lining pen, line the eyes, nose and freckles, outline and stitch everything. Glue button to apron.

4. **PILGRIM BOY**
   Paint collar and boots **Light Ivory**. Splatter lightly with **Bambi Brown**. Paint face and hands **Fleshtone**. Shirt, pants and hat are **Nightfall**. Paint elbow patch and hat band **Caucasian Flesh**. Stipple cheeks **Gypsy Rose**. Using black lining pen, outline and stitch everything. Glue on buttons. Thread a large button onto 15 inches of wire. Wrap wire around a pencil and thread ends through the holes in hands. Tie 15 inches of jute into a bow and glue to hand.

5. **LEAF**
   Paint entire leaf **Wedgewood Green**. Stipple outside edges and veins in **Caucasian Flesh**. Patch is **Nightfall** with **Light Ivory** heart. Spatter lightly with **Light Ivory**. Using a black lining pen, line and stitch everything, including small black hearts.

6. **ACORN**
   Bottom of acorn is **Nightfall**. Top of acorn and the large comma stroke and dot are **Light Ivory**. Paint stem and line plaid lines on top of acorn **Caucasian Flesh**. Small hearts are **Nightfall**. Splatter lightly with **Light Ivory**. Using black lining pen, line and stitch everything, make three dot design on top of acorn.

FINISHING ALL PIECES

1. Spray with finishing spray/varnish.
2. Hang all pieces on tree with 18 inches of jute.
3. Decorate tree by wrapping with fabric, gluing on fabric and raffia bow and buttons on base (optional).
4. Tree topper remains unpainted except for the letters "Thankful Hearts Welcome Here" in **Nightfall**. Dot ends of letter **Nightfall**. Line bow and make three dot design in black lining pen.

THANKSGIVING TREE

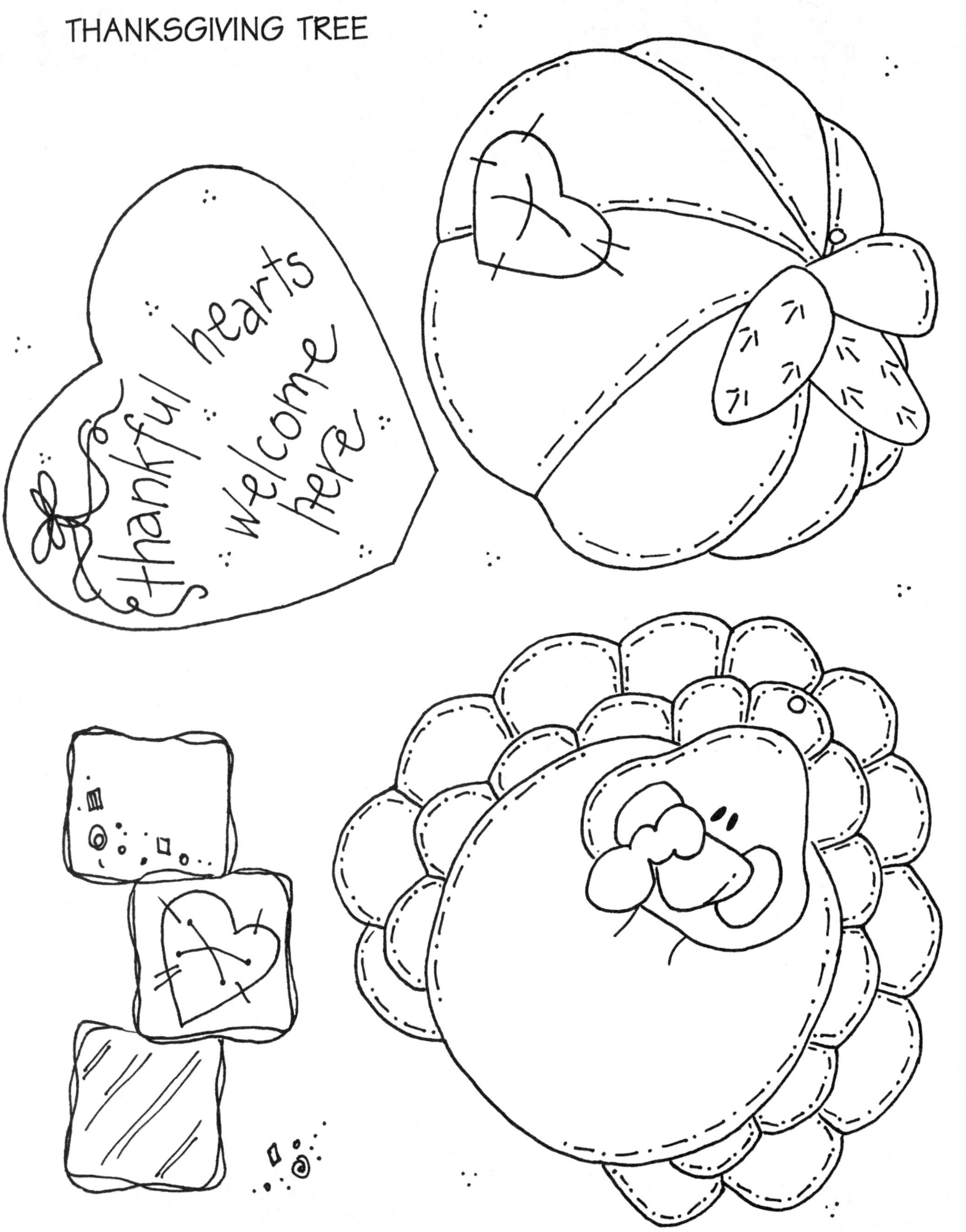

Never Pass up an opportunity to tell someone you love them.

BUTTONS TURKEY

This pattern is dedicated to Hannah Moe, whose brief life touched many and taught us to love and give thanks.

PALETTE - Delta Ceramcoat

Light Ivory	Cape Cod	Nightfall	White
Black	Caucasian Flesh	Cayenne	Bambi Brown
Dresden Flesh			

MISCELLANEOUS SUPPLIES

Buttons (optional)   Natural Raffia   Fabric Scrap

NOTE: Please refer to the fold-out page for painting patterns.

1. **Light Ivory:** Paint entire turkey body piece.
2. **Nightfall:** Paint feet.
3. **Bambi:** Splatter turkey body piece.
4. **Cape Cod** and **Nightfall:** Alternating colors, paint back row feathers.
5. **Caucasian Flesh** and **Cayenne:** Alternating colors, paint front row of feathers.
6. **Light Ivory:** Lightly splatter both rows of feather and feet.
7. **Cayenne:** Paint waddle.
8. **White:** Paint eyes.
9. **Caucasian Flesh:** Paint cheeks.
10. **Bambi:** Paint beak.
11. **Cape Cod:** Paint hat.
12. **Dresden Flesh:** Paint hat brim.
13. **Black:** Dot pupils.
14. **Light Ivory:** Stroke and dot small design on hat.
15. Lightly sand edges.
16. **Black Lining Pen:** Line/stitch and dot everything.
17. Spray with varnish.
18. Glue turkey together. Glue feet to body. Glue front row feathers behind body and center back row feathers behind front row feathers. Before glue sets, stand upright so all pieces are flat across the bottom. Glue on buttons (optional). Make a bow out of raffia and glue on body. Tie fabric strip into bow and glue on top of raffia bow.

PAINTING "GIVE THANKS" BLOCKS

Block No. 1: Paint **Caucasian Flesh.** Lightly sand edges. Paint the patch **Dresden Flesh.** The heart on top of patch is **Nightfall.** The detail lines on heart are **Dresden Flesh.** Line and stitch in black lining pen. Spray with finishing spray/varnish.

Block No. 2: Paint **Nightfall.** Sand edge lightly. Line "Give Thanks" in **Dresdent Flesh.** Line and stitch in pen. Spray with finishing spray/varnish.

Block No. 3: Paint **Dresdent Flesh.** Sand edges lightly. Line "gobble" and line and stitch around outside edge in black lining pen. The dots at the ends of the letters are **Caucasian Flesh.** Spray with finish spray/varnish, then glue on buttons.

THANKSGIVING TURKEY

PALETTE - Delta Ceramcoat

Antique White   Forest Green
Leprechaun   Cayenne
Caucasian Flesh   Butter Yellow
Burgundy Rose   Medium Flesh
Black

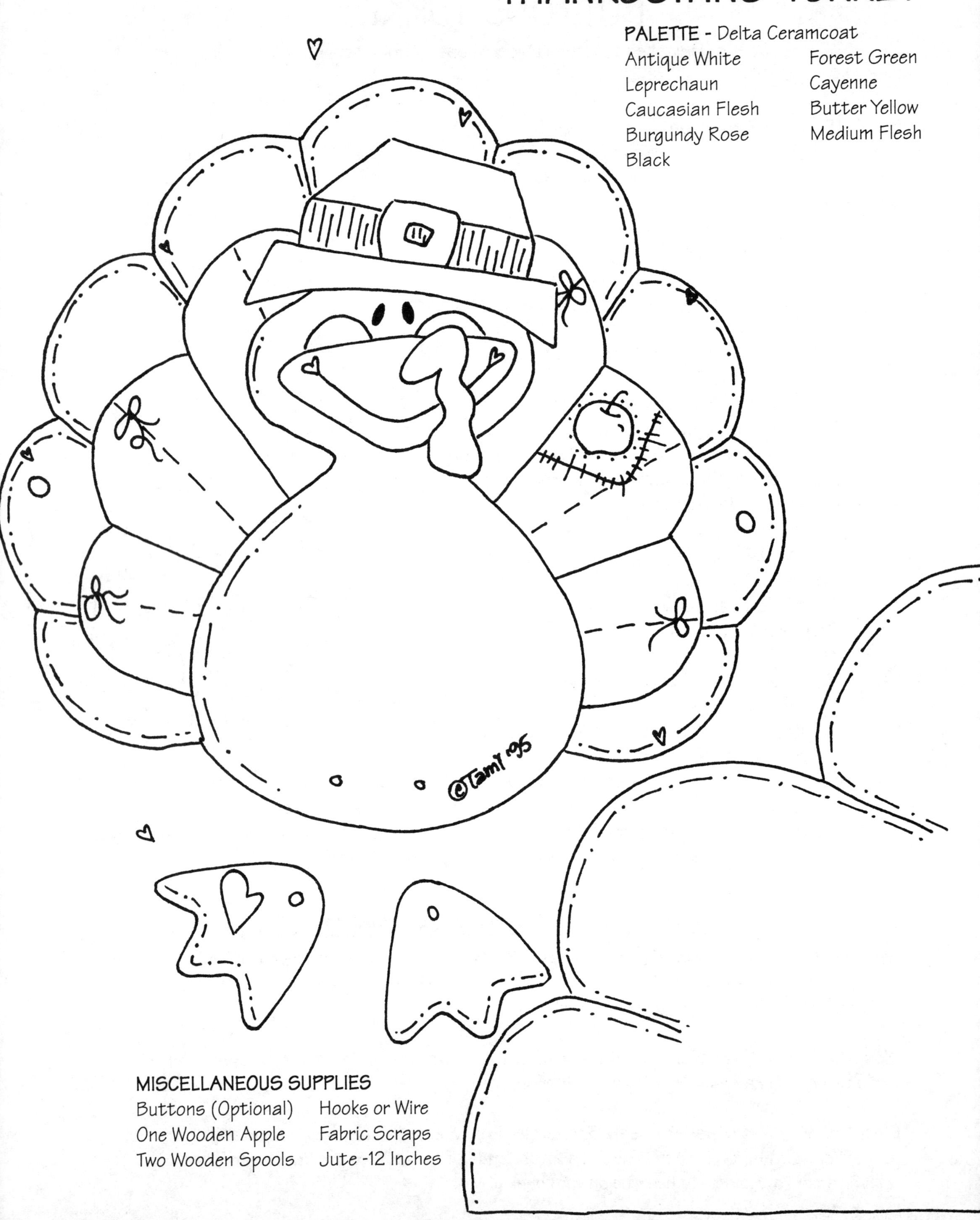

MISCELLANEOUS SUPPLIES

Buttons (Optional)   Hooks or Wire
One Wooden Apple   Fabric Scraps
Two Wooden Spools   Jute -12 Inches

"COME IN FOR A SPELL" WITCH
cut doily
Come in
for a spell!

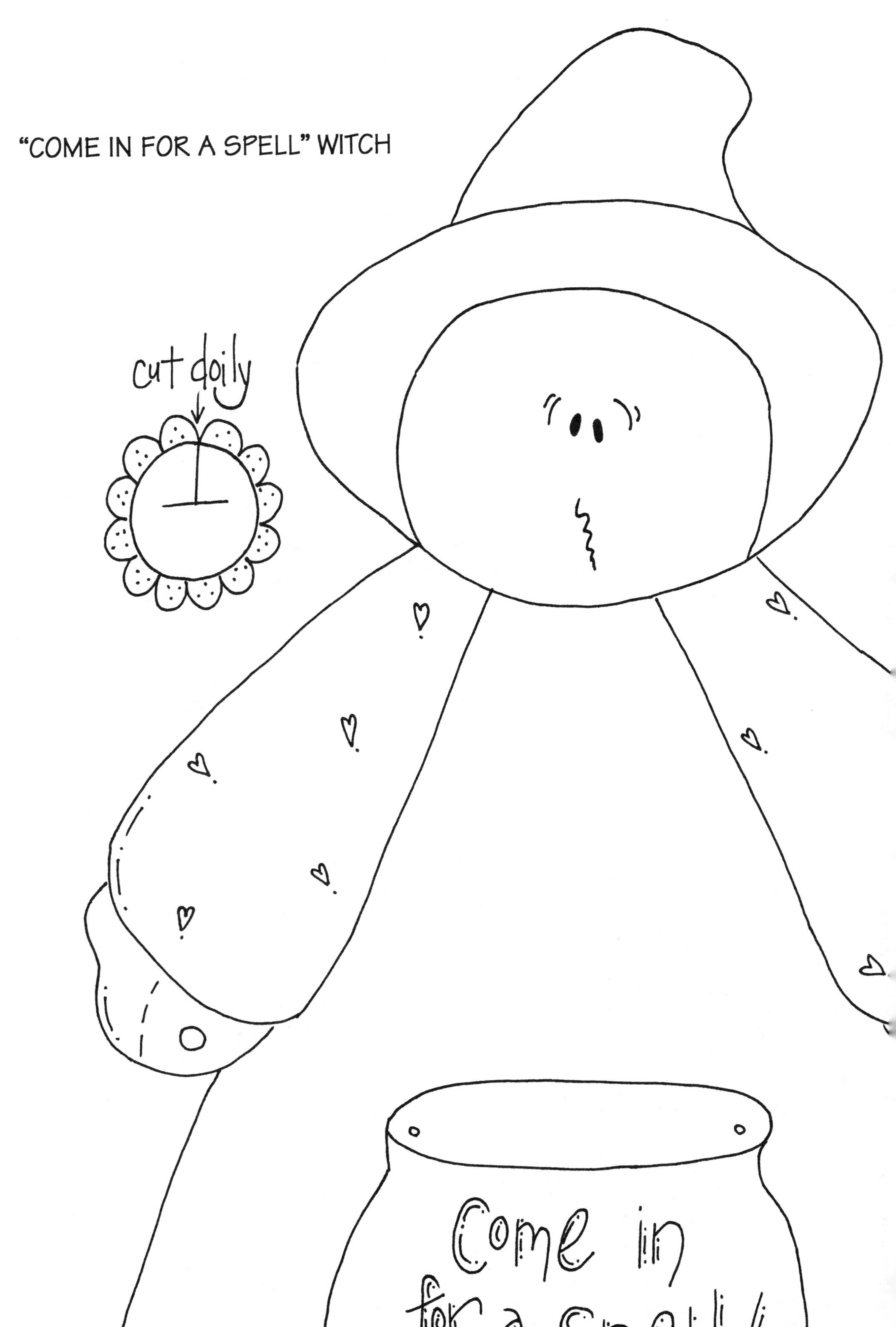

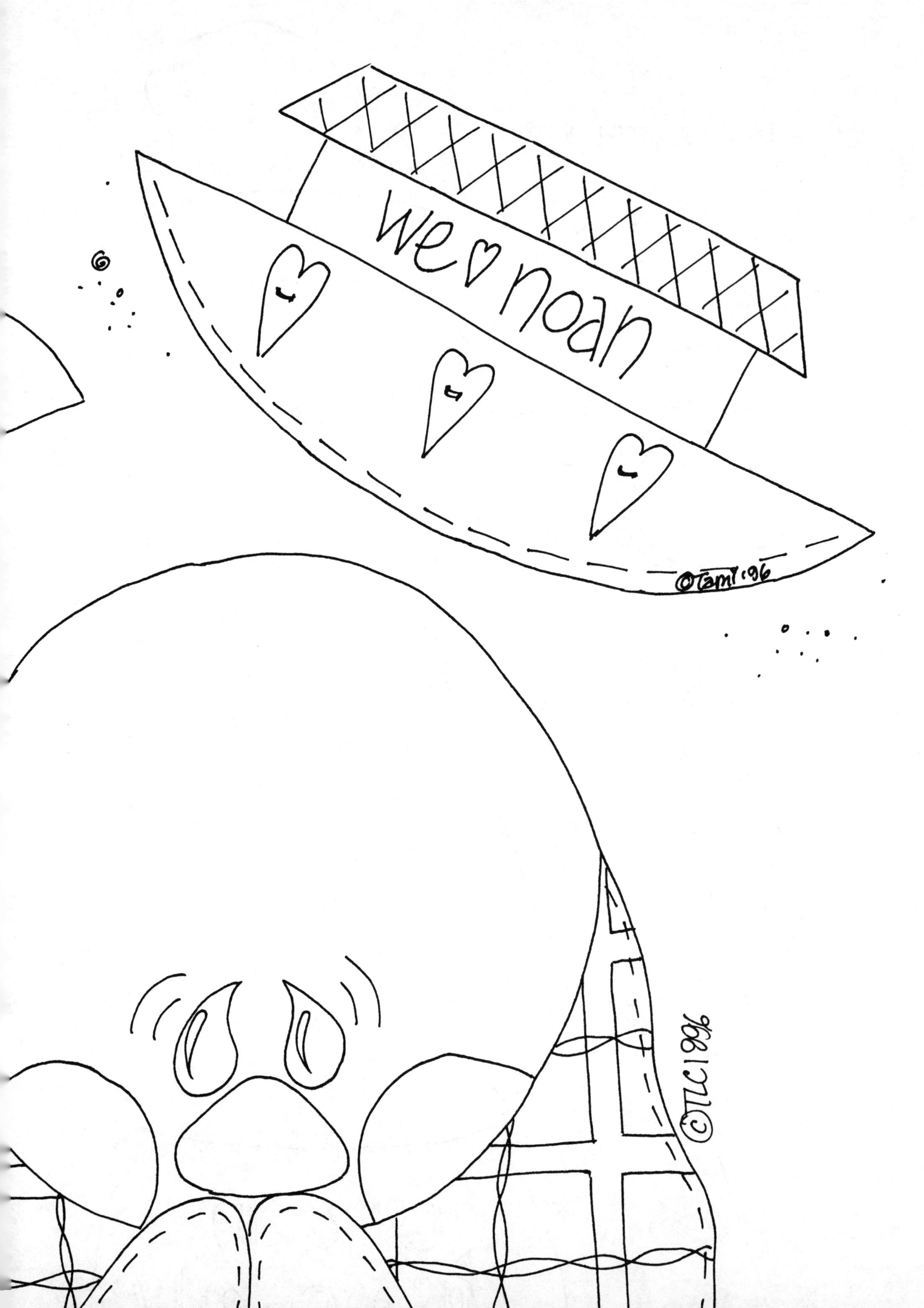

we ♥ noah
©tami.96
©TLC1996

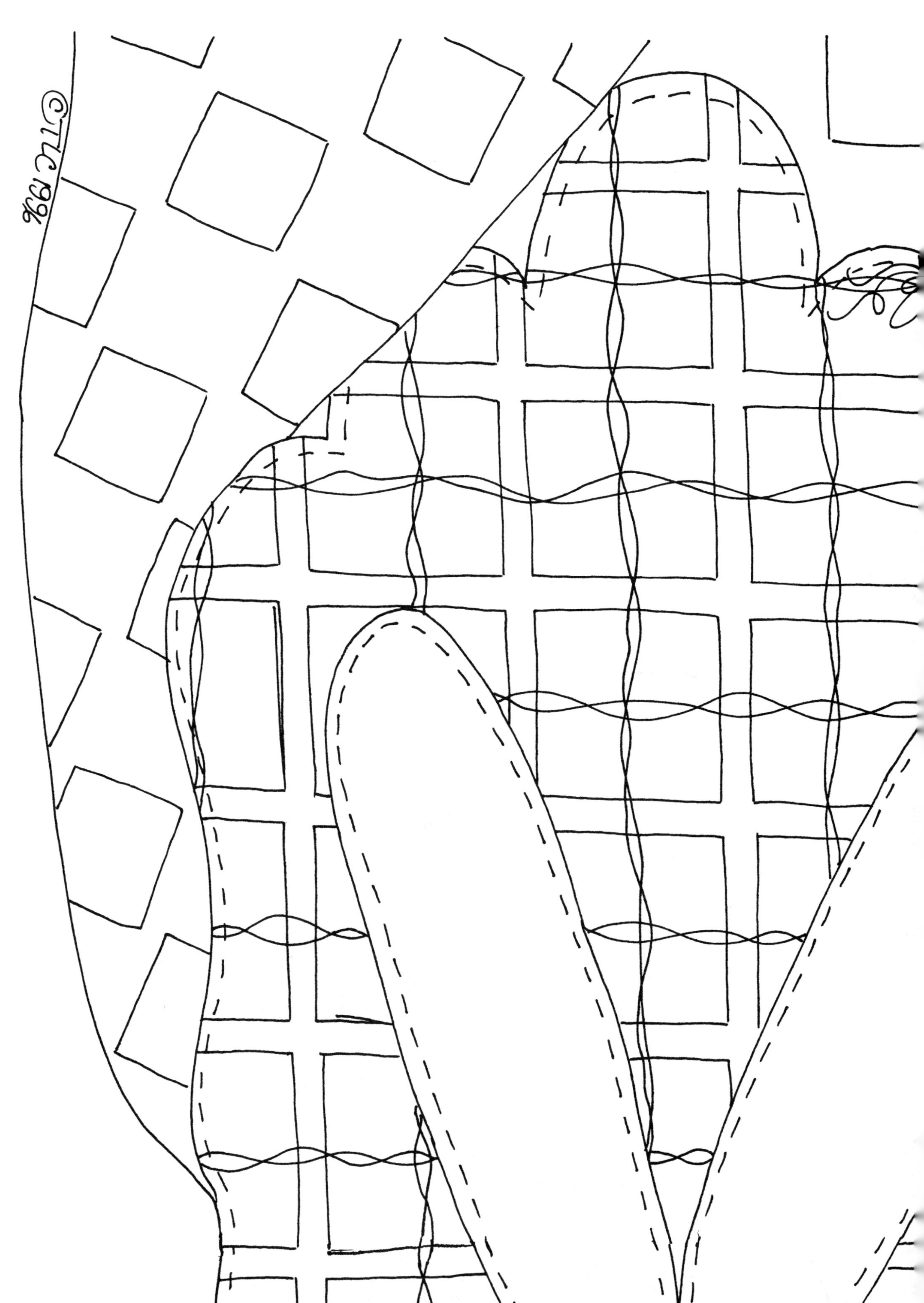

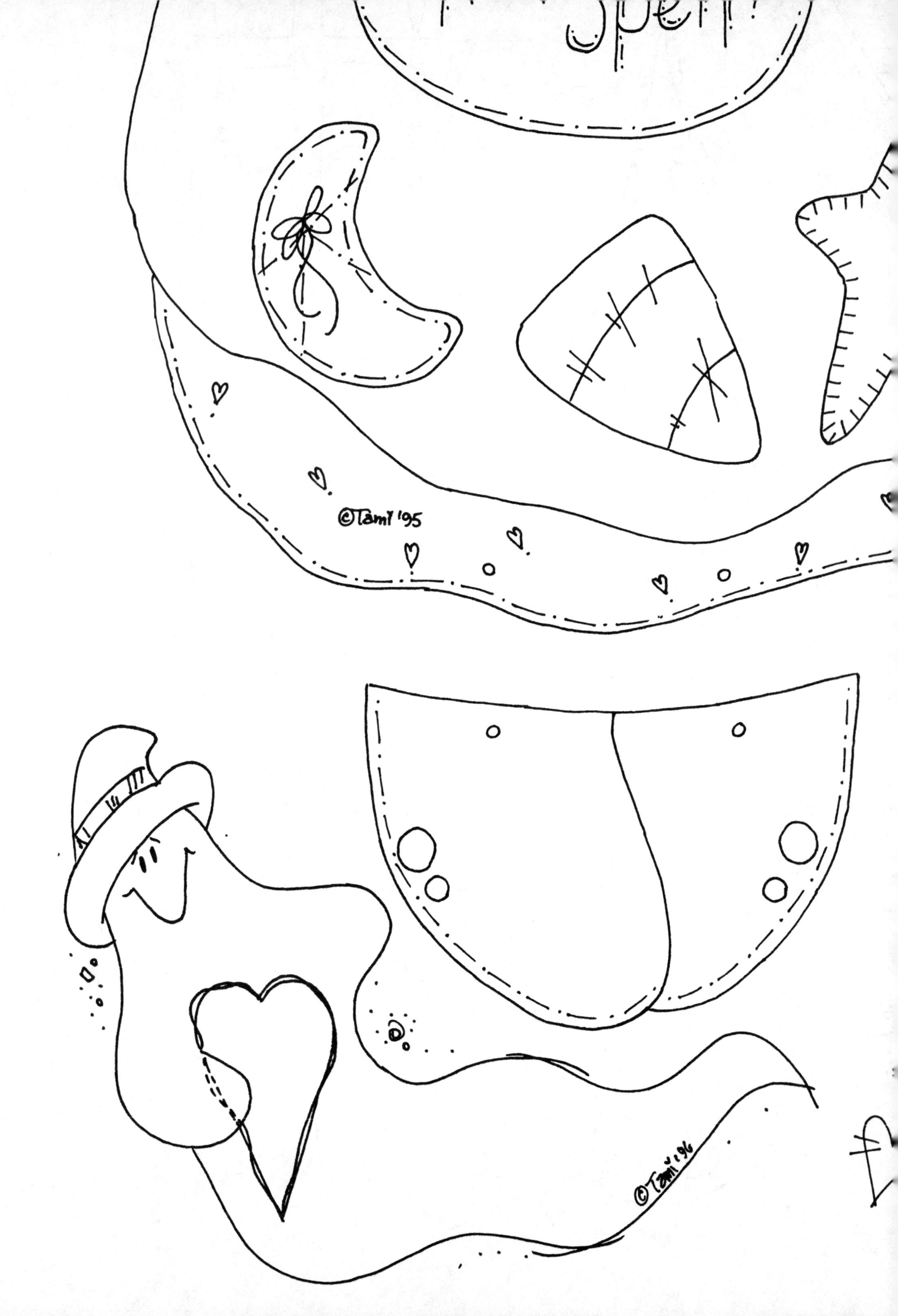

©Tami '95
©Tami '96

gobble
back row feathers –
left

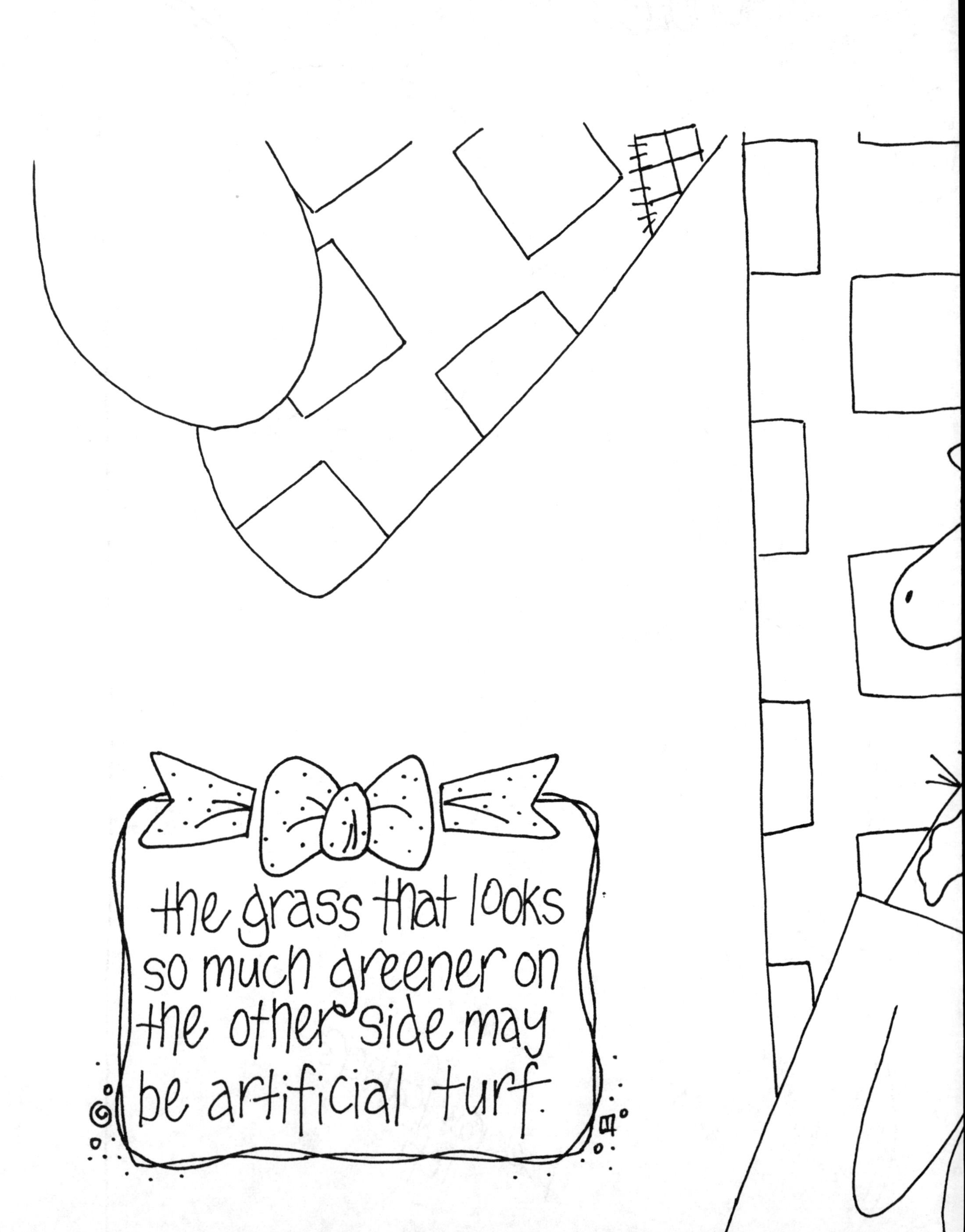

the grass that looks
so much greener on
the other side may
be artificial turf

GINGERBREAD HOUSE

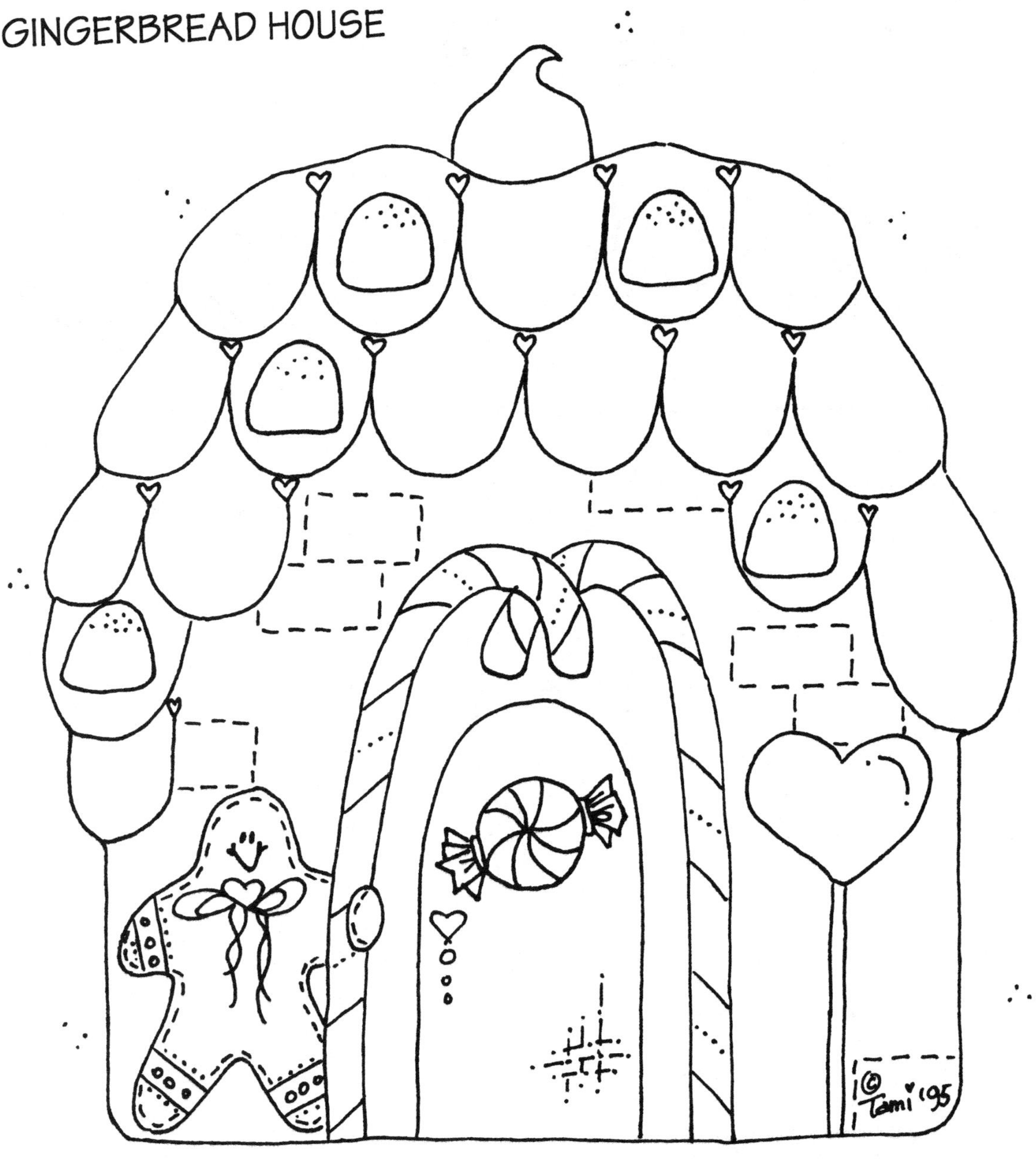

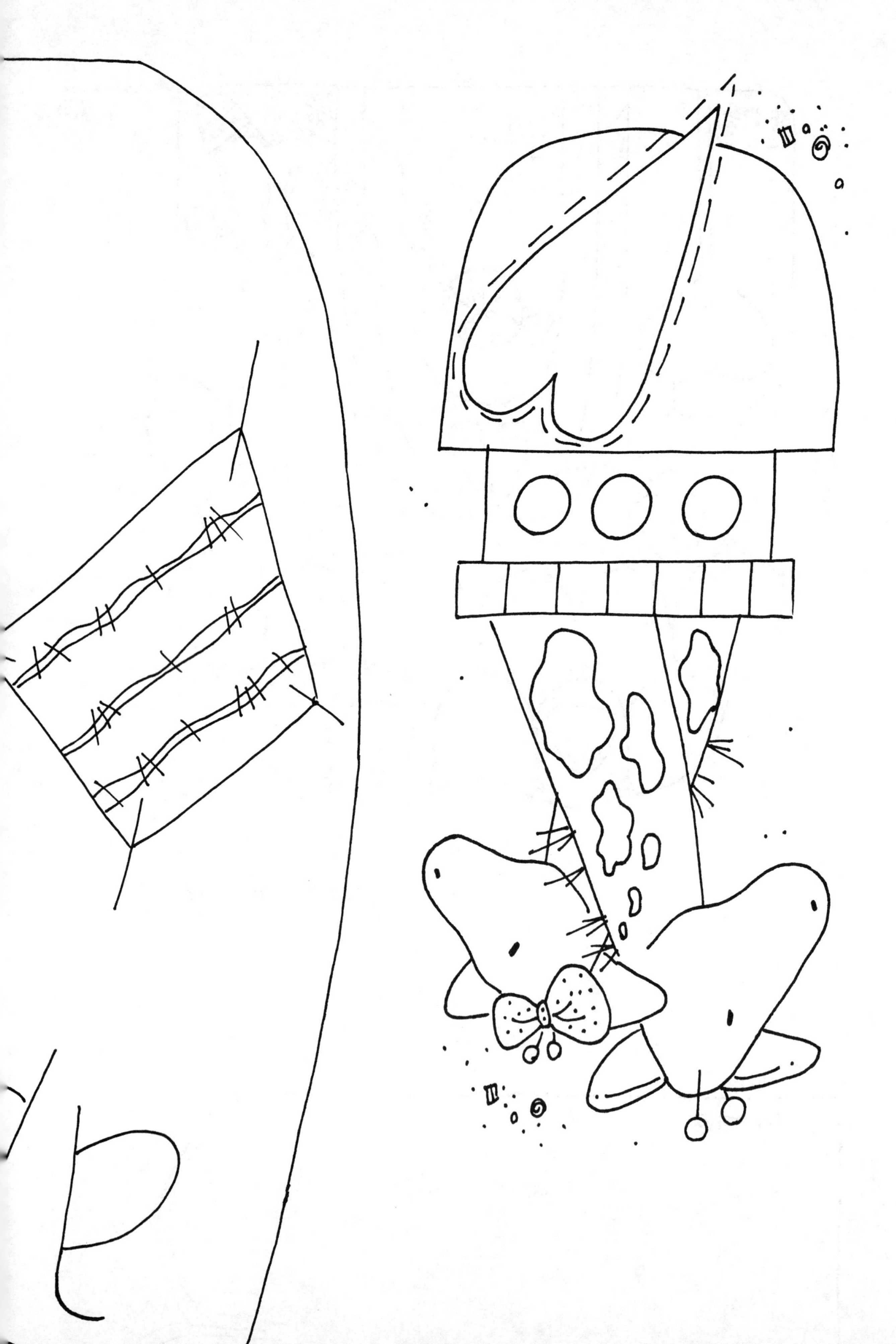

THANKSGIVING TURKEY Cont.

1. **Antique White:** Paint body of turkey.
2. Alternating **Forest Green** and **Leprechaun,** paint back row of tail feathers.
3. Alternating **Cayenne** and **Caucasian Flesh,** paint front row of tail feathers.
4. **Caucasian Flesh:** Paint feet.
5. **Butter Yellow:** Paint beak and buckle on hat.
6. **Burgundy Rose:** Paint waddle, hat band, heart on left foot, wooden apple and hearts on ends of mouth.
7. **Medium Flesh:** Paint cheeks.
8. **Black:** Paint hat.
9. **Antique White:** Stipple lightly on all tail feathers and feet. Paint patch and both spools. Lightly splatter wooden apple.
10. **Burgundy Rose:** Paint apple on patch.
11. Black Lining Pen: Line/stitch everything.

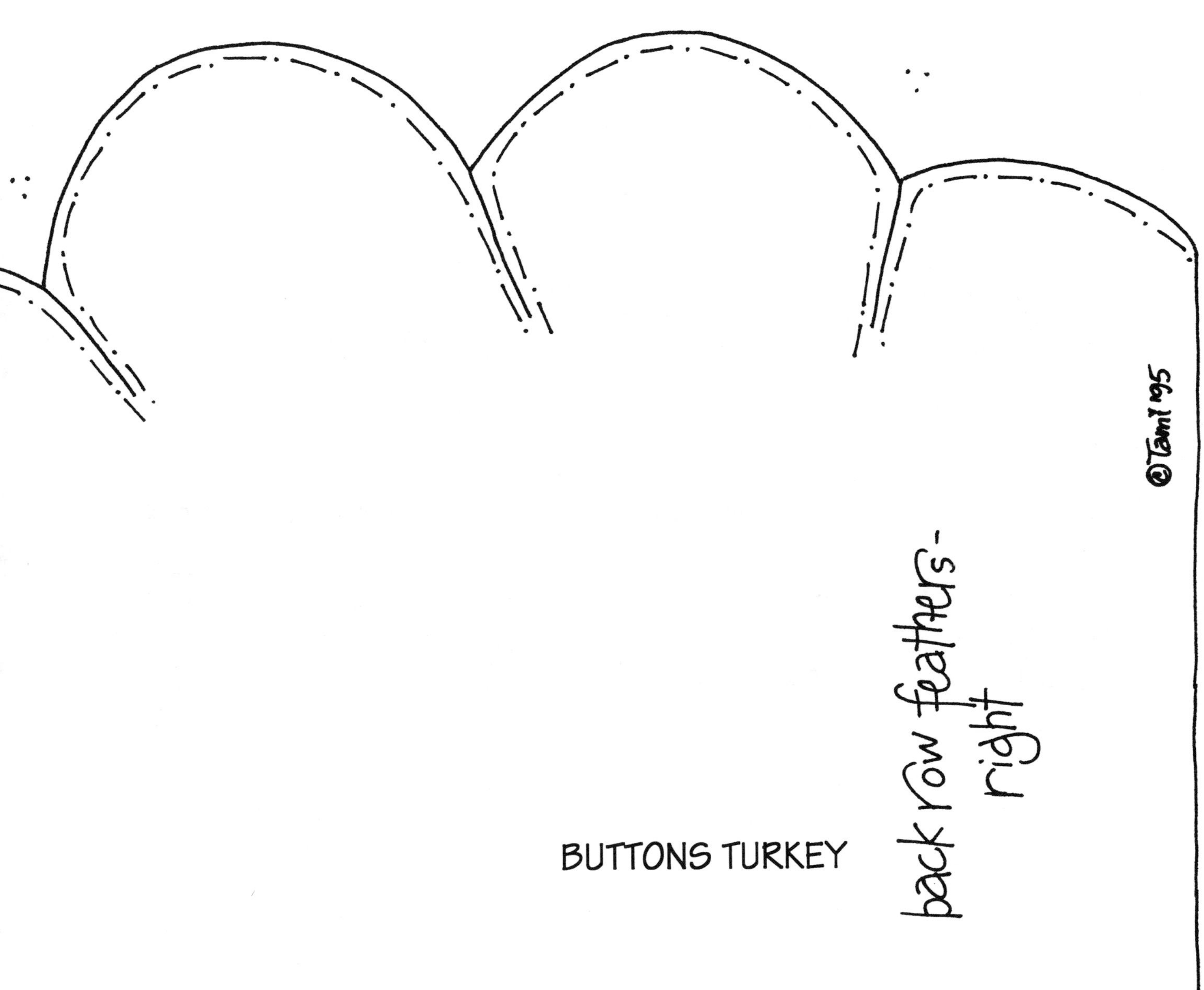

PEEK-A-BOO GHOST

PALETTE - DELTA CERAMCOAT

Lichen Gray	Pumpkin	Leprechaun	Wisteria
Bambi	Black	Orange	White
Vintage Wine	Forest Green		

MISCELLANEOUS SUPPLIES

Buttons (optional)	Natural/Orange Raffia	Wire or Hooks

NOTE: Please refer to the fold-out page for painting pattern.

1. **Lichen Gray:** Paint entire piece.
2. **Pumpkin:** Paint pumpkin.
3. **Leprechaun:** Paint leaves on pumpkin.
4. **Wisteria:** Paint bow on pumpkin.
5. **Bambi:** Paint stem.
6. **Vintage Wine:** Shade bow.
7. **Forest Green:** Shade leaves.
8. **Black:** Paint eyes, nose and mouth on pumpkin.
9. **Orange:** Line the pumpkin.
10. White Wash Ghost: Be careful to paint the wash on evenly. It's better to have the paint a little too watered down and need to paint a second coat. You can always add more paint but it's hard to "take away" with a wash. We want the ghost to look transparent and still be able to see the pumpkin underneath that ghostly hug!
11. **White:** Highlight around all outside edges of ghost.
12. Black Lining Pen: Line everything that isn't underneath ghost. Line ghost's eyes, mouth, and eyebrows.
13. **Orange:** Stipple cheeks lightly.
14. Spray varnish.
15. Glue on buttons and raffia.
16. Attach twisted wire or hooks for hanging from one of the Country Welcome Signs or Bird-house Stand!

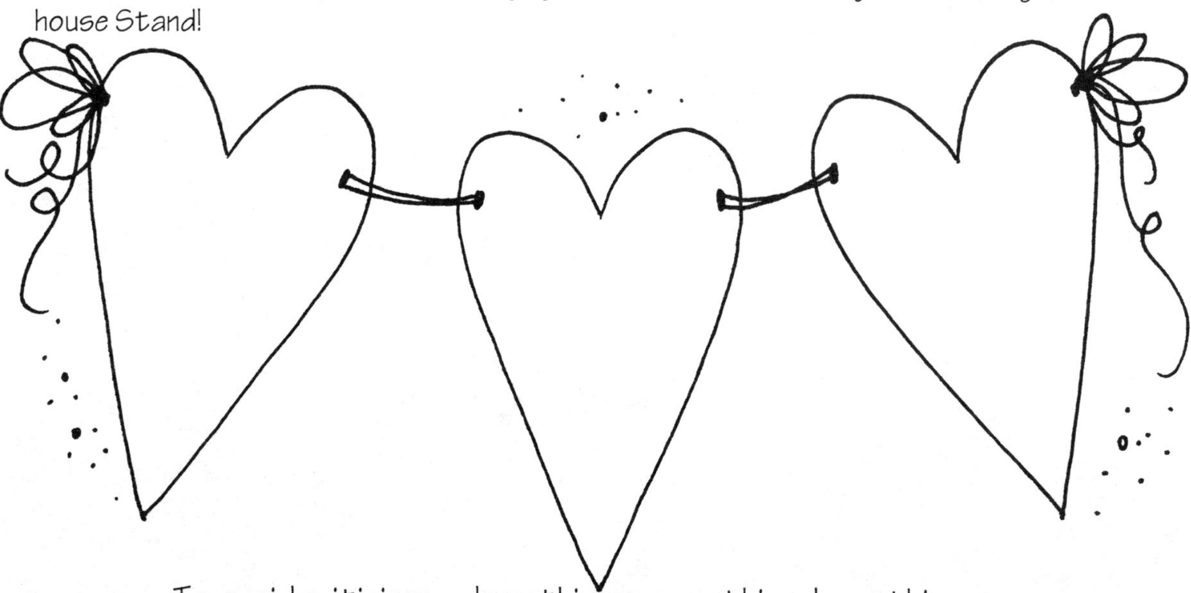

To avoid criticism... do nothing, say nothing, be nothing.

BAT'S HAVE HEART

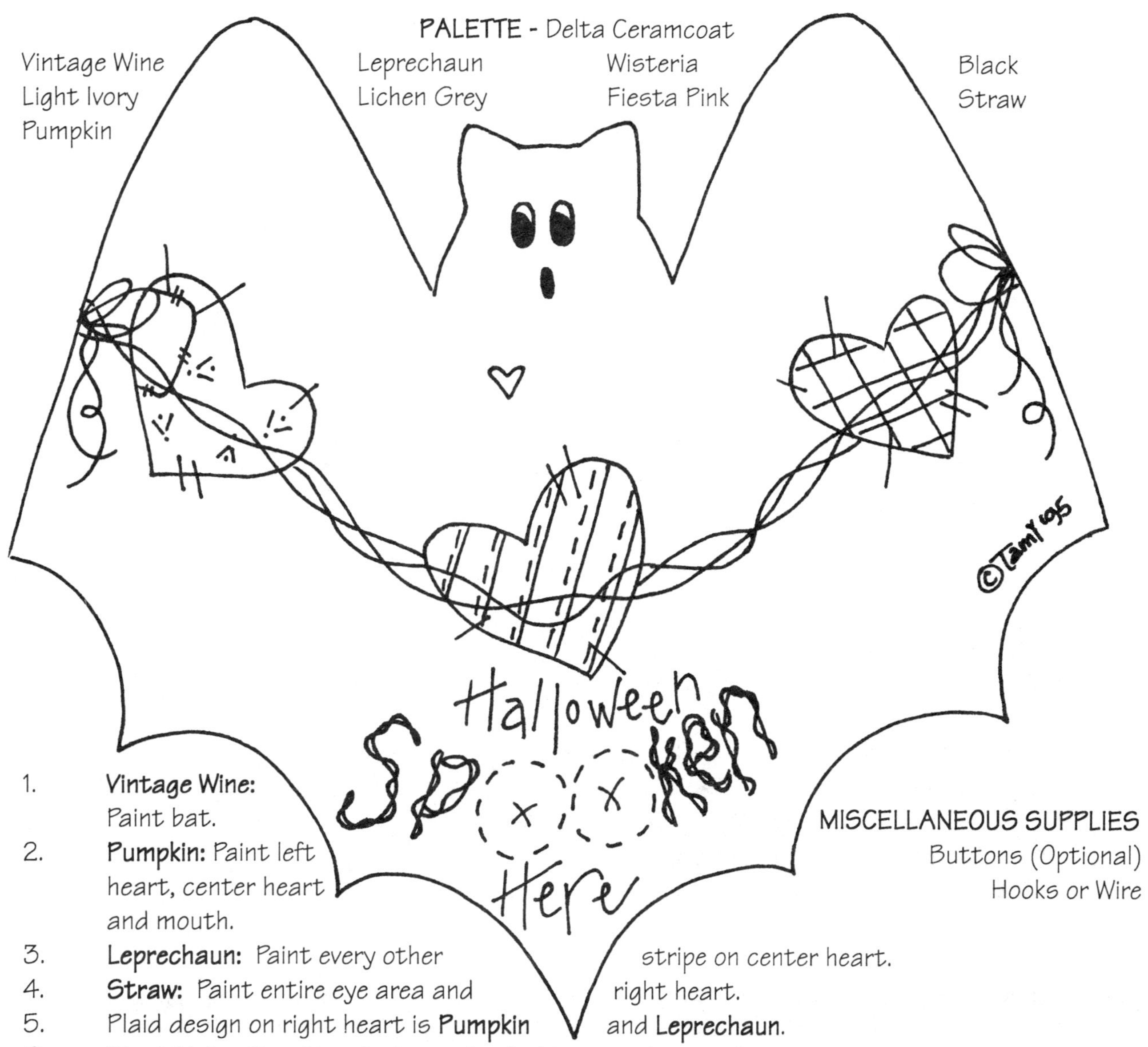

1. **Vintage Wine:** Paint bat.
2. **Pumpkin:** Paint left heart, center heart and mouth.
3. **Leprechaun:** Paint every other stripe on center heart.
4. **Straw:** Paint entire eye area and right heart.
5. Plaid design on right heart is **Pumpkin** and **Leprechaun.**
6. Black Lining Pen: Line design and stitching on other two hearts.
7. **Wisteria:** Stipple highlights on top of wings, ears, and here and there on bat. Paint patch on left heart.
8. **Light Ivory:** Strengthen highlights on top of wings and ears.
9. **Fiesta Pink:** Stipple cheeks softly and paint small heart below mouth.
10. **Straw:** Line letters.
11. **Lichen Grey:** Line the flowing lines through and around hearts, bows on sides, and wavy lines around letters.
12. **Black:** Dot pupils in eyes.
13. Black Lining Pen: Line long stitches on hearts.
14. Spray with varnish.
15. Glue on buttons.
16. Attach wire or hooks for use on one of the Country Welcome Signs or Birdhouse Stand!

MISCELLANEOUS SUPPLIES
Buttons (Optional)
Hooks or Wire

THANKSGIVING TURKEY Cont.

12. Bend approximately 16 inches of wire (for the legs) in half, thread through the holes in the turkey body from the back. Twist wire around end of a brush. Thread ends through the holes in the feet and wrap ends around the wire legs to secure. Twist approximately 3-1/2 inches of wire for the stem. Glue one end into apple.
13. Spray all pieces with finishing spray/varnish.
14. Glue fabric scraps around wooden spools. Using jute, thread a spool, the apple, then the other spool. Thread through holes in the turkey and securely knot jute on the back. Secure with a dab of glue on the back. Glue on buttons (optional).
15. Attach twisted wire or hooks for use on a Country Welcome Sign or Birdhouse Stand!

"HARVEST BLESSINGS" SCARECROW

PALETTE - Delta Ceramcoat

Antique White	Burgundy Rose	Forest Green	Butter Yellow
AC Flesh	Bambi Brown	Black	Gypsy Rose

MISCELLANEOUS SUPPLIES

Spanish Moss	Natural colored Raffia	Buttons (Optional)

1. **Antique White:** Paint face and neck cloth, birdhouse, and patch on left side.
2. **Burgundy Rose:** Paint every other check on shirt, roof of birdhouse, nose, gloves and lines under eyes.
3. **Forest Green:** Finish painting every other check on shirt.
4. **Butter Yellow:** Paint hat and sunflower on birdhouse. Paint top patch on right side.
5. **AC Flesh:** Paint board and center of sunflower. Shade face and neck cloth, birdhouse and patch on left side.
6. **Bambi Brown:** Paint birdhouse door, the underneath patch on right side. Shade board and hat.
7. **Black:** Paint eyes and bird. Line mouth.
8. **Antique White:** Lightly stipple highlights on hat, dot eye on bird. Dot the dots on the yellow patch.
9. **Gypsy Rose:** Paint beak on bird, stipple cheeks on bird and scarecrow, paint heart on cheek and on bird.
10. **Black:** Dot pupil in bird's eye.
11. **Bambi Brown:** Paint dots in center of sunflower.
12. **Forest Green:** Paint heart on board.
13. **Black:** Line the Letters HARVEST BLESSINGS on board.
14. Black lining pen: Line/stitch everything.
15. Spray with finishing spray/varnish.
16. Glue moss on the scarecrow's forehead. Glue on buttons (optional). Glue raffia on the sides.
17. Attach hooks or twisted wire for use on a Country Welcome Sign or Birdhouse Stand.

"HARVEST BLESSINGS" Scarecrow

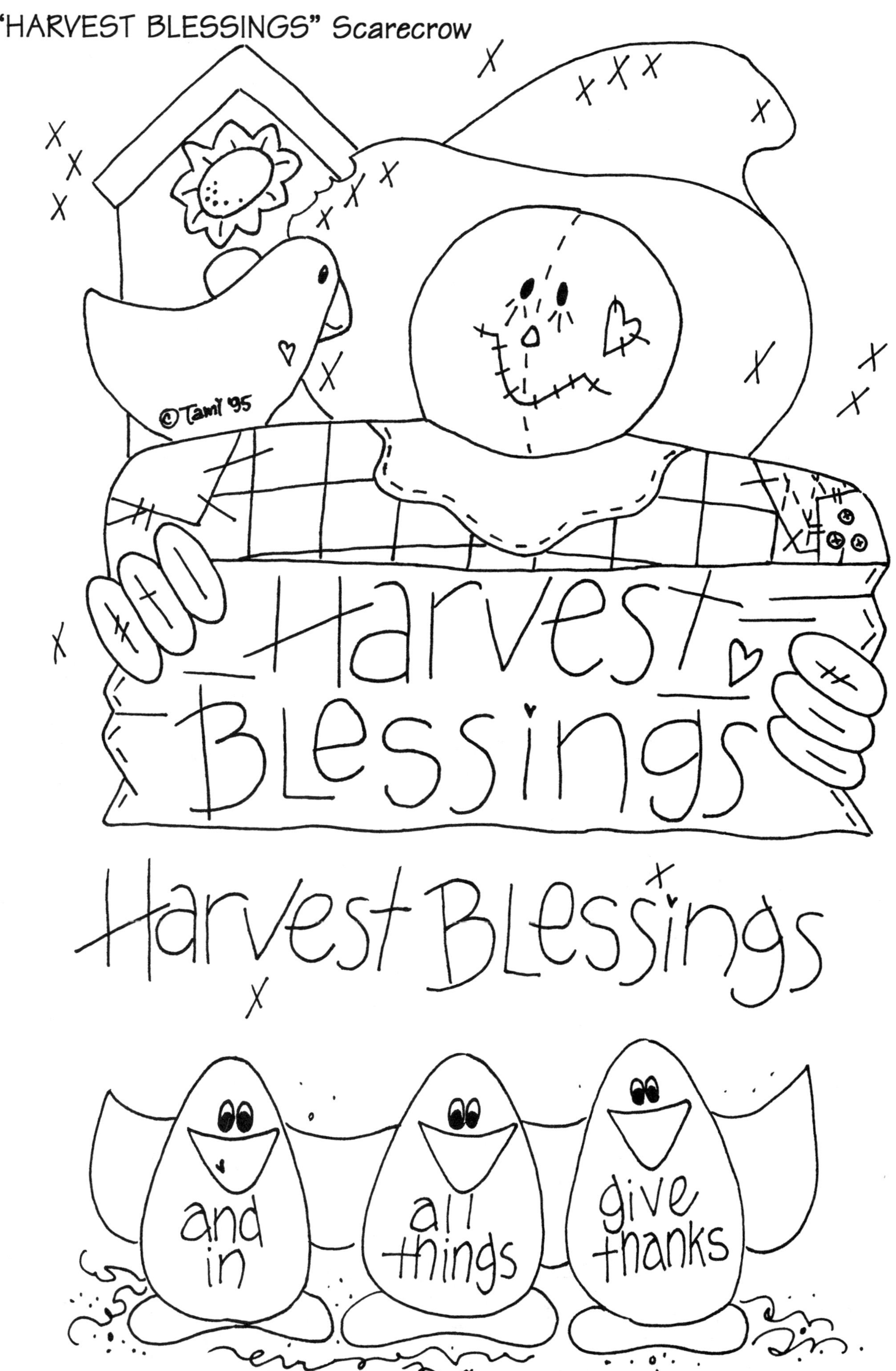

HALLOWEEN CLAY POT

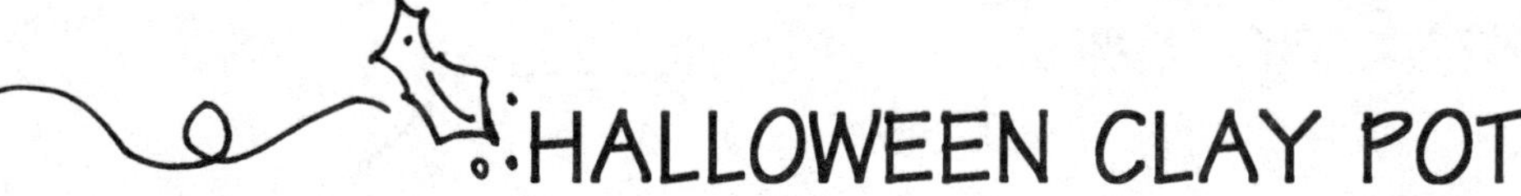

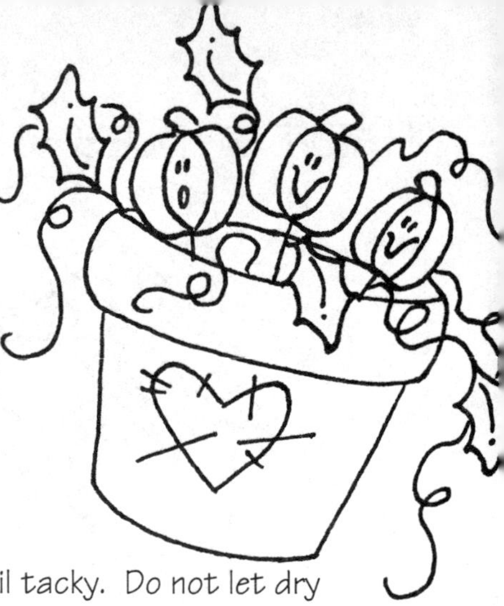

PALETTE - Delta Ceramcoat

Cadet Gray	Pumpkin
Butter Yellow	Black
Light Ivory	

SUPPLIES

Delta Crackle
Six Inch Clay Pot
Raffia

1. **Pumpkin:** Paint rim of clay pot.
2. **Cadet Gray:** Paint bottom of pot.
3. Using crackle, paint whole pot using even, heavy strokes. Let dry until tacky. Do not let dry completely.
4. **Black:** Paint entire pot.
5. After it's dry, paint one light coat of **Butter Yellow** for moon.
   Candy Corn: Top end is **Light Ivory**. Middle is **Pumpkin**. Large end is **Butter Yellow**.
   Star is **Pumpkin**.
6. Spray varnish.
7. Glue raffia around pot and make a bow.

NOTE: This Halloween pot is quick and eay to make! Fill with Halloween candy for the Trick-or-Treaters or give as a gift to the hostess of a Halloween party. You could have a Halloween pot sitting on your desk at work or give to the Teacher in your life for her desk at school!

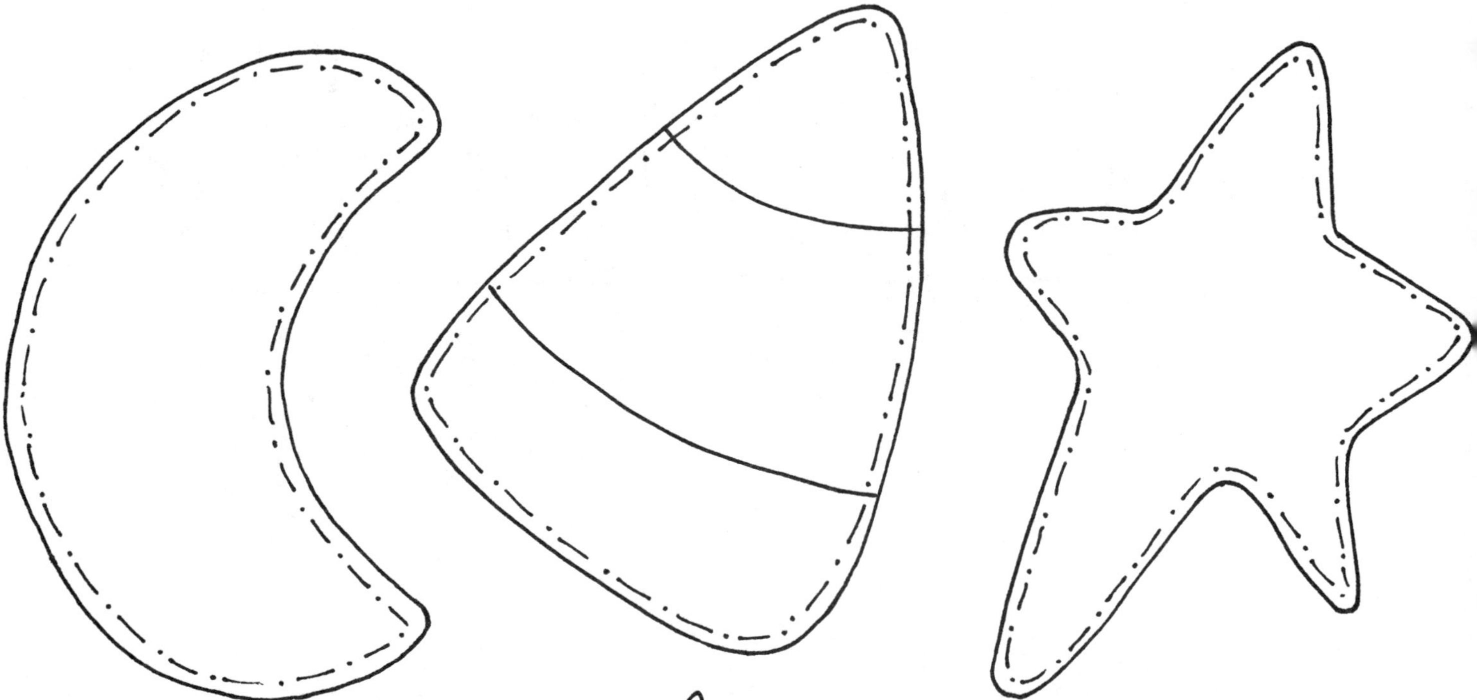

"COME IN FOR A SPELL" WITCH

PALETTE - Delta Ceramcoat

Fleshtone	Sunbright Yellow	Light Ivory	Pumpkin
Charcoal	Cadet Gray	Dusty Plum	Medium Flesh
Orange	Golden Brown	Bambi Brown	Napa Wine
Persimmon Pink			

MISCELLANEOUS SUPPLIES

Six inch fabric	Battenburg Lace Doily, tea dyed	Raffia	Wire
Purple Netting	Spanish Moss	Jute	

NOTE: Please refer to the fold-out page for painting patterns.

1. **Fleshtone:** Paint face and hands.
2. **Sunbright Yellow:** Paint sleeves and bottom of dress, moon, large end on candy corn.
3. **Light Ivory:** Paint small end of candy corn.
4. **Pumpkin:** Paint star and center of candy corn.
5. **Charcoal:** Paint hat and pinafore.
6. **Cadet Gray:** Paint caldron.
7. **Dusty Plum:** Paint shoe.
8. **Medium Flesh:** Shade face and hands.
9. **Orange:** Shade star, center of candy corn.
10. **Golden Brown:** Shade sleeves, bottom of dress, top of candy corn and moon.
11. **Napa Wine:** Shade shoes.
12. **Bambi Brown:** Shade small end of candy corn.
13. **Dusty Plum:** Stipple highlights on pinafore and hat.
14. **Charcoal:** Stipple shading on caldron. Float shade across opening of caldron. Splatter shoes lightly.
15. **Pumpkin:** Dot hearts and sleeves and bottom of dress.
16. **Sunbright Yellow:** Paint dots on sides of each shoe.
17. **Persimmon Pink:** Stipple cheeks.
18. **Light Ivory:** Highlight eyes with dots. Line letters on caldron.
19. **Black Lining Pen:** Line/stitch everything, eyes, mouth.
20. Spray with finishing spray/varnish.
21. **Wire:** Two pieces 10-12 inches long, twist and wrap around hands and caldron, threading a button on one side. Add orange raffia and jute bow, buttons to feet and star and jute to hang feet. Glue Spanish Moss hair and purple netting bow on hat.

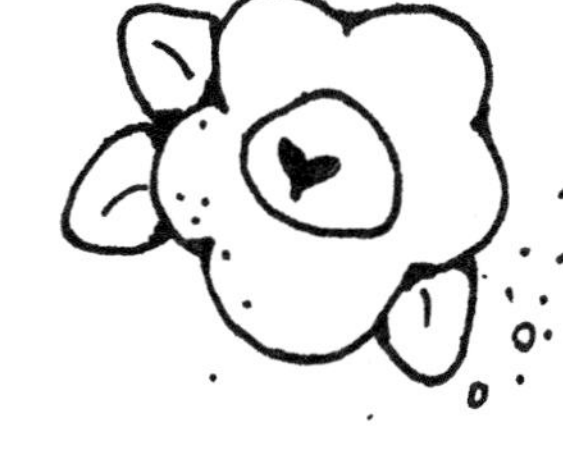

PAINTING PUMPKIN ON COLLAR

1. **Pumpkin:** Paint entire pumpkin piece.
2. **Orange:** Shade pumpkin.
3. **Bambi:** Paint stem.
4. **Wedgewood Green:** Line vines.
5. **Black:** Paint eyes, nose and mouth.
6. **Black Lining Pen:** Stitch around edge.
7. Glue pumpkin to collar.

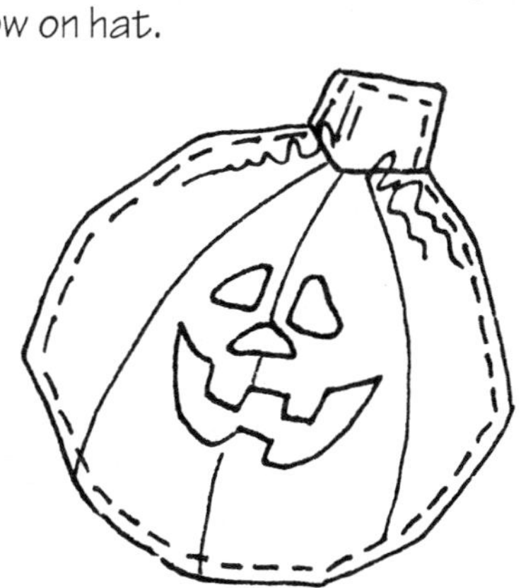

SHAMROCK

PALETTE - Delta Ceramcoat

Forest Green	Wedgewood Green	Black
Light Ivory	Butter Yellow	Bambi Brown

MISCELLANEOUS SUPPLIES

Buttons	One Wooden Flower Shaped Button
Wire or Hooks	Three Fabric Pieces, each approximately 4 Inches Square
Black Floss/Heavy Thread	

PAINTING SHAMROCK

Heart No. 1 - Squares are **Forest Green** and **Wedgewood Green**. Line a thin plaid line of **Butter Yellow** through center of each square.

Heart No. 4 - Paint birdhouse flower wooden button **Light Ivory**. Paint background **Wedgewood Green**. Shade around outside **Forest Green**. Line stem and leaves **Forest Green**. Using **Forest Green**, shade outside edge of heart, line stem and leaves, paint roof of birdhouse. Paint birdhouse holes **Black**. Paint squares on birdhouse roof and center of flower wooden button in **Butter Yellow**.

Heart No. 2 - Paint background **Light Ivory**. Shade **Bambi Brown**. Heart is **Forest Green**. Checks are **Black**, **Bambi Brown** and **Wedgewood Green**.

Heart No. 3 - Stripes are **Wedgewood Green** and **Forest Green**. Paint "good luck" **Black**. Highlight lines are **Light Ivory**.

FINISHING SHAMROCK

1. Lightly splatter **Light Ivory**.
2. Black Lining Pen: Line/stitch everything.
3. Sand edges lightly.
4. Spray with varnish.
5. Tie buttons with black floss if desired.
6. Glue on buttons.
7. Making fabric windsock streamers: Cut each piece of fabric according to circular pattern. Trim from top if shorter length is desired. Hold the three fabric streamer pieces by the tops, glue together, then glue to shamrock.
8. Attach twisted wire or hooks to hang from one of the Country Welcome Signs or Birdhouse Stand. Happy St. Patrick's Day!

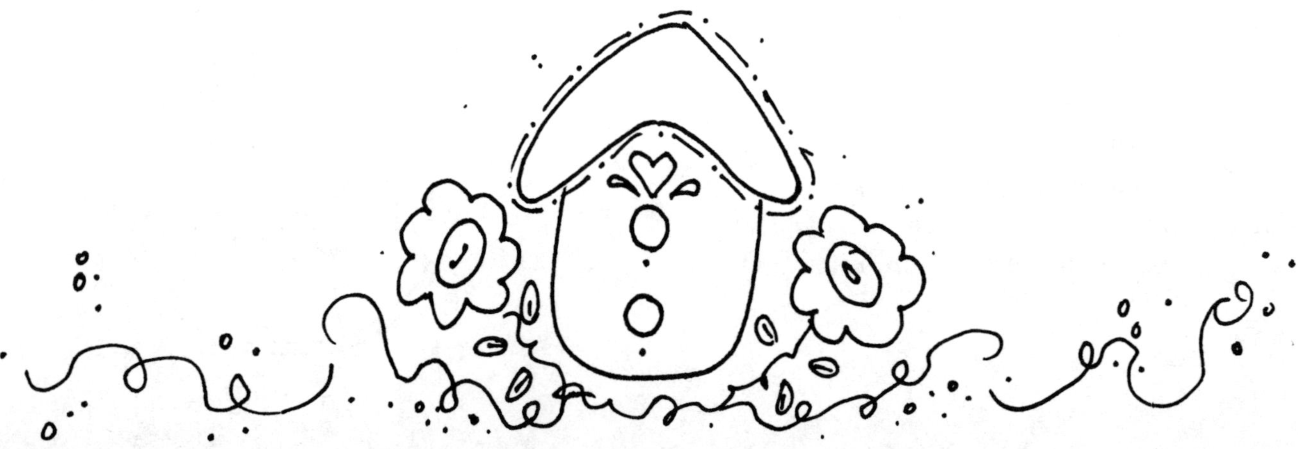

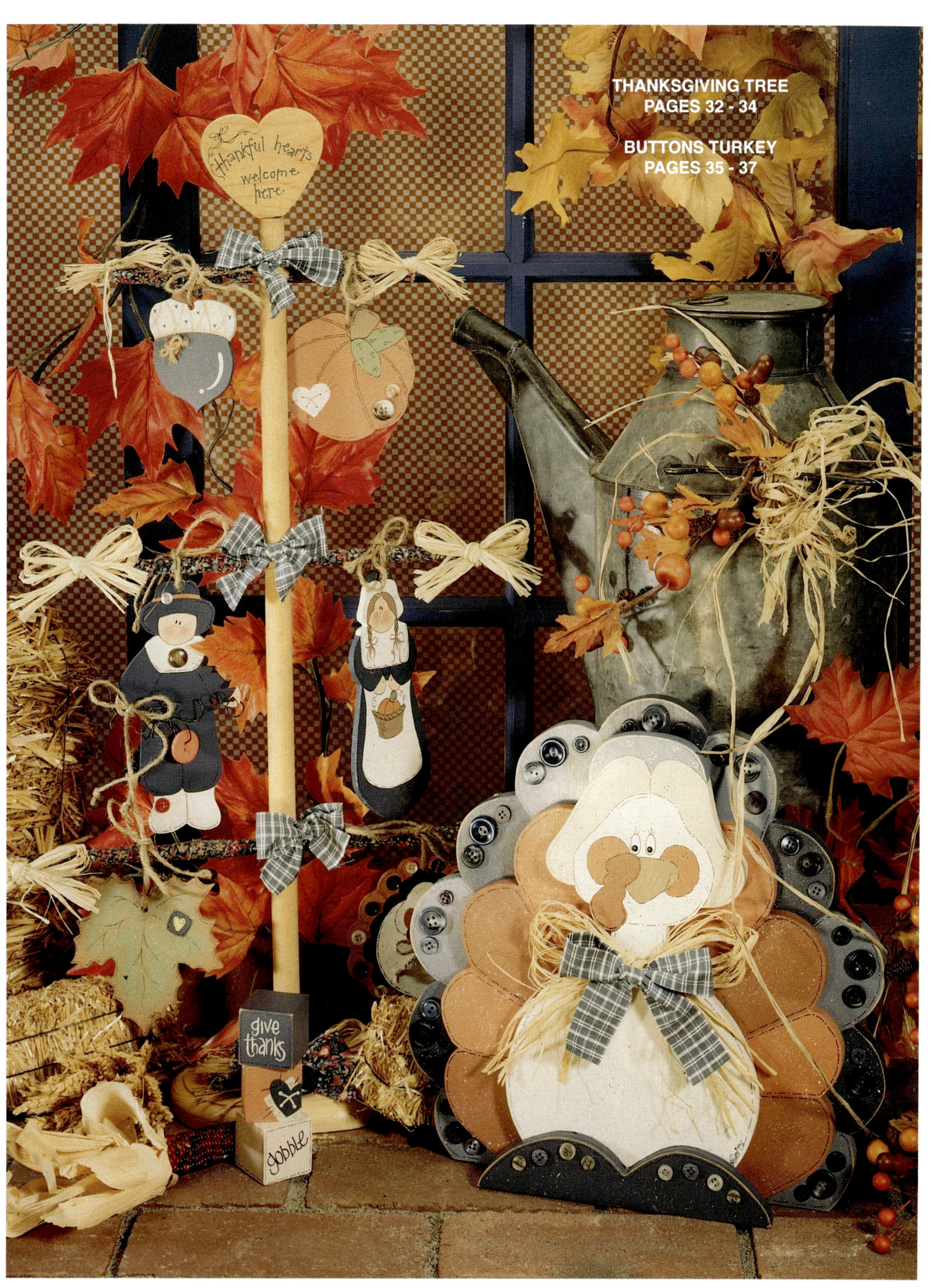

THANKSGIVING TREE
PAGES 32 - 34

BUTTONS TURKEY
PAGES 35 - 37

thankful hearts
welcome
here

give
thanks

gobble

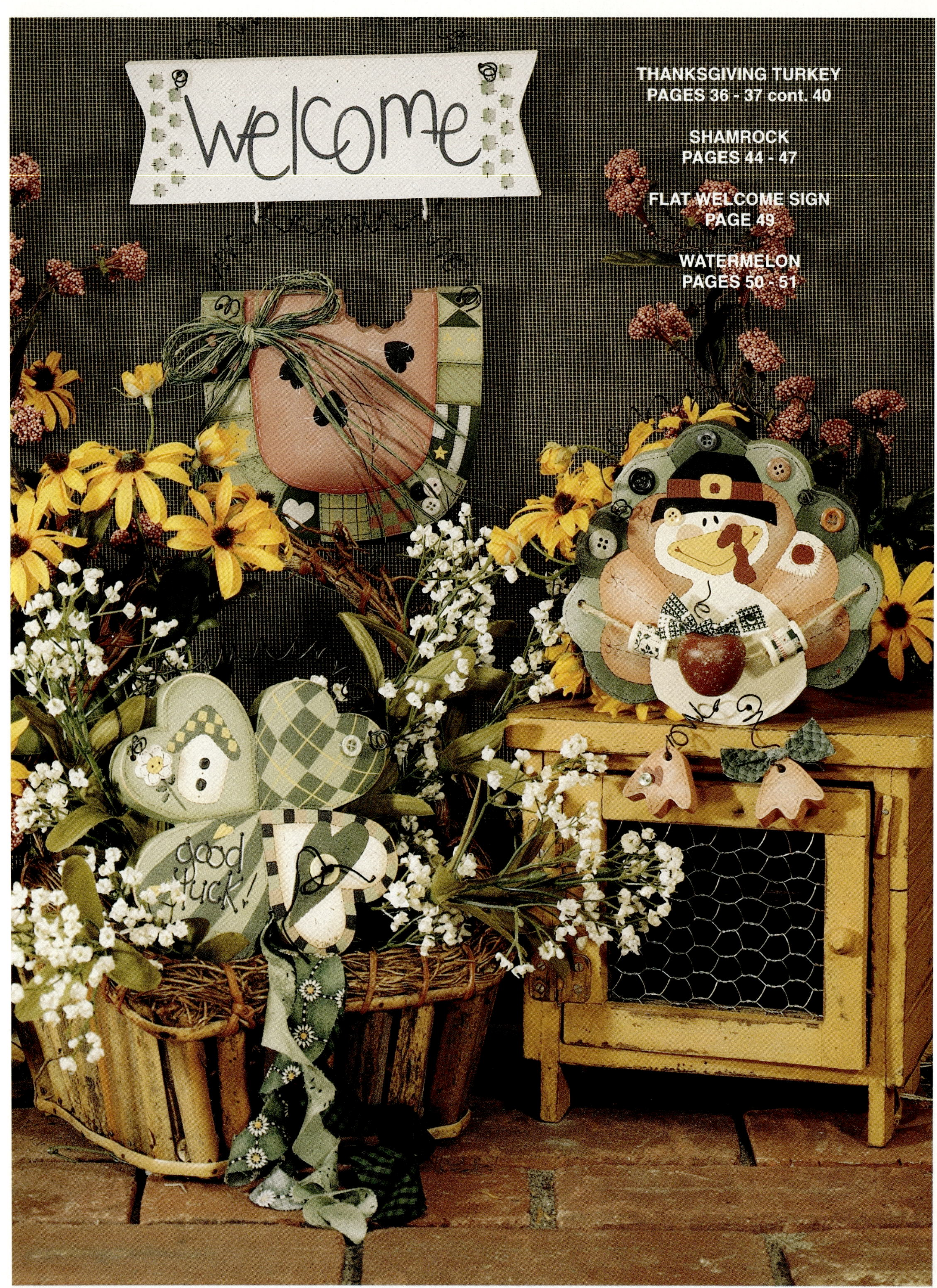

Welcome

THANKSGIVING TURKEY
PAGES 36 - 37 cont. 40

SHAMROCK
PAGES 44 - 47

FLAT WELCOME SIGN
PAGE 49

WATERMELON
PAGES 50 - 51

good luck!

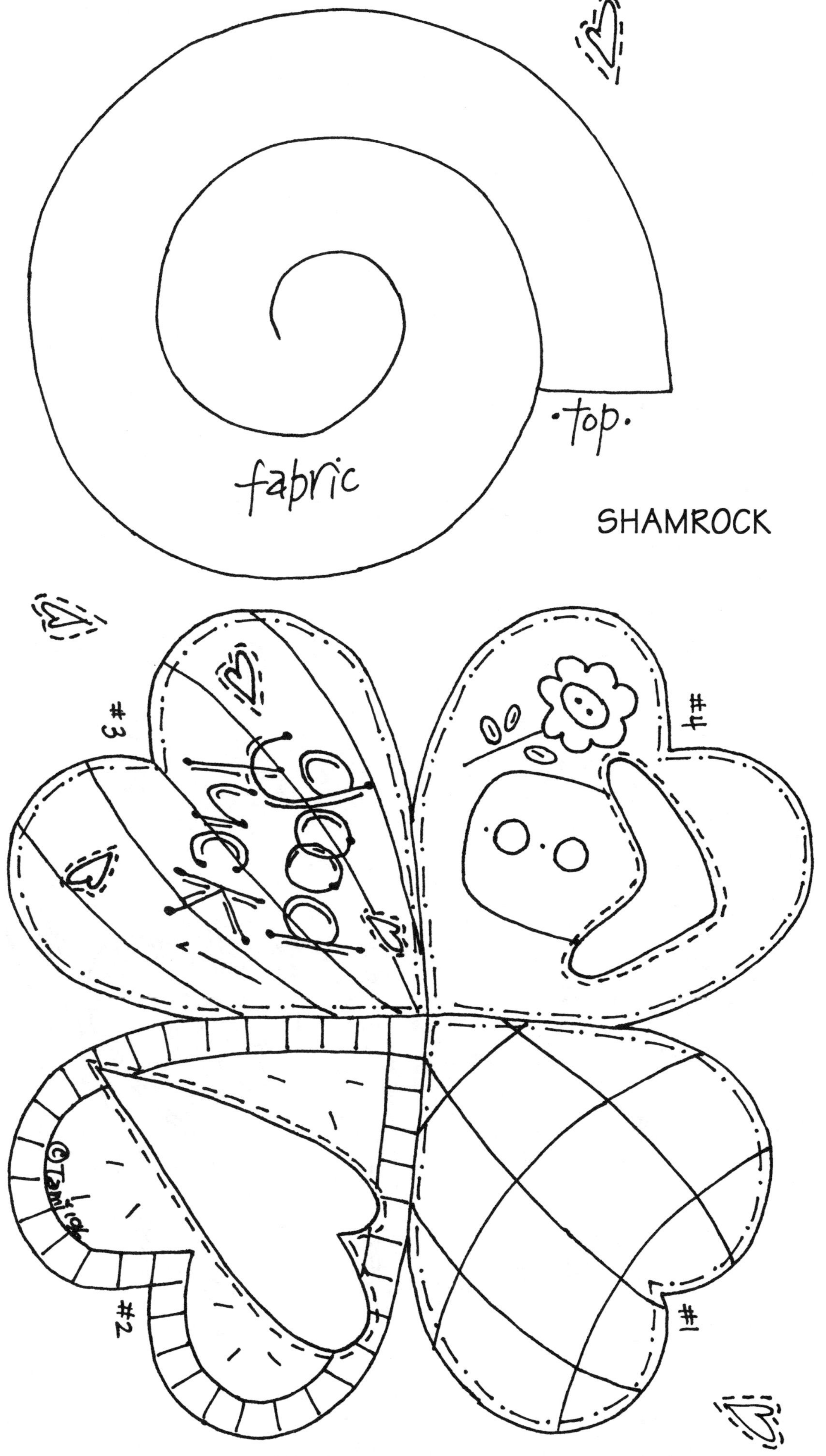

fabric
·top·
SHAMROCK
#3
#4
#2
#1
©Tami

BIRTHDAY CUPCAKE

PALETTE - Delta Ceramcoat

Burnt Umber Sachet Pink
Antique Rose Bambi Brown
Light Ivory Butter Yellow

MISCELLANEOUS SUPPLIES

Buttons
Wire or Hooks

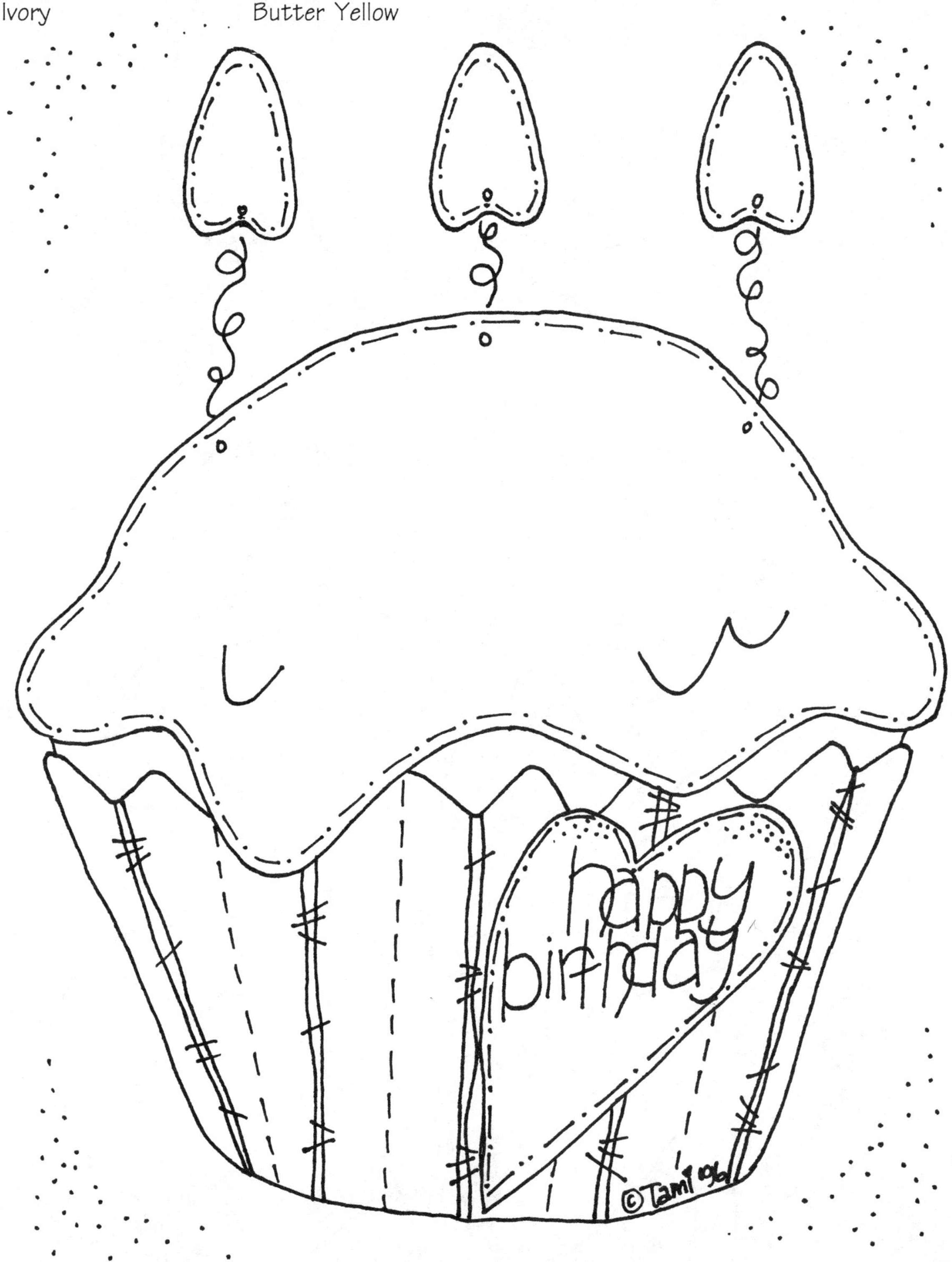

IDEA:

It would be cute to cut out extra hearts and individualize each heart with someone's name in place of the button there! (i.e. "Happy Birthday, Aimee"--etc.). You could make the hearts interchangeable by using a small piece of hook and latch tape glued on and/or small staples or nails.

BIRTHDAY CUPCAKE Cont.

1. **Burnt Umber:** Add water to paint so it's real thin, making a wash. Paint entire piece.
2. **Sachet Pink:** Paint frosting.
3. **Antique Rose:** Paint heart, shade frosting.
4. Mix equal parts of **Bambi Brown** and **Light Ivory** together. Using this mixture, paint cupcake paper cup.
5. **Butter Yellow:** Paint flames.
6. **Burnt Umber:** Shade cupcake under frosting.
7. **Bambi Brown:** Shade cupcake paper cup.
8. **Light Ivory:** Highlight cupcake paper cup and top of frosting. Highlight top of heart. Lightly splatter all pieces.
9. **Black Lining Pen:** Line letters. Line/stitch everything
10. Spray varnish.
11. Glue on buttons.
12. Cut wire in two pieces approximately 12 inches long. Connect flames to cupcake by inserting wire through holes and twisting it around a pencil or brush handle.
13. Attach hooks or wire from top of the two outer flames to hang from one of the Country Welcome signs or Birdhouse Stand.

FLAT WELCOME SIGN

This Welcome Sign is perfect for that little country accent that you can change to fit your every mood!

PALETTE - Delta Ceramcoat

White	Cactus Green	Green Sea
Cape Cod	Nightfall	

1. **White:** Paint entire piece.
2. **Cape Cod:** Splatter lightly.
3. **Cactus Green:** Paint checks.
4. **Green Sea:** Shade left side of checks.
5. **Nightfall:** Line letters.
6. Black Lining Pen: Stitch the checks.
7. Spray with varnish.
8. Screw in hooks and wire to finish.

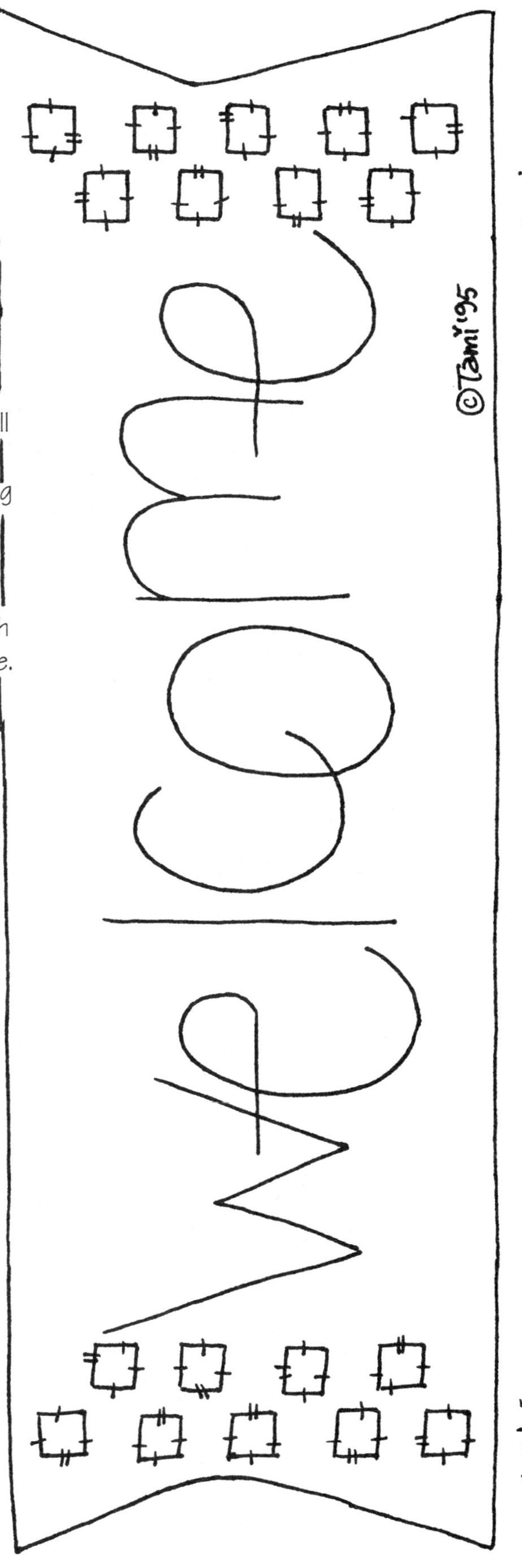

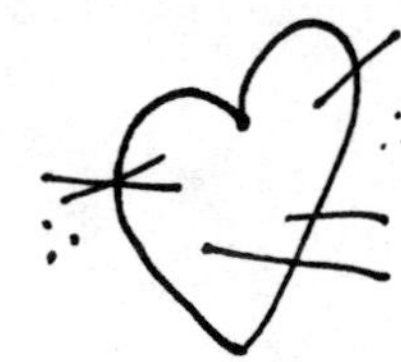
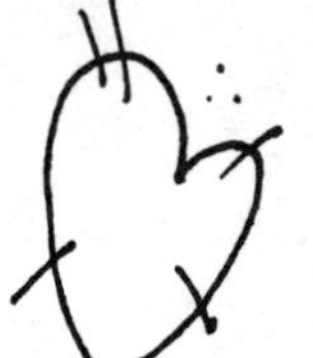
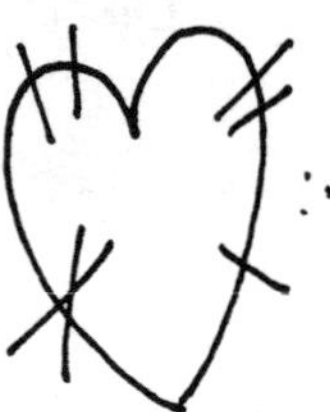

WATERMELON

PALETTE - Delta Ceramcoat

Gypsy Rose	Dusty Mauve	Stonewedge Green	Light Ivory
Forest Green	Butter Yellow	Wedgewood Green	Bambi Brown
Black	Charcoal	Village Green	Blue Wisp

PAINTING WATERMELON

Paint center of Watermelon **Gypsy Rose**. Shade **Dusty Mauve**, stipple highlight **Light Ivory**. Heart seeds are **Charcoal**. Line stitching close to rind and around seeds.

1. Square No. 1: Paint **Wedgewood Green**. Shade **Forest Green**. Line **Gypsy Rose**.
2. Square No. 2: Paint **Forest Green**. Hearts are **Gypsy Rose**.
3. Square No. 3: Paint **Village Green**. Shade **Forest Green**. Line design **Light Ivory**.
4. Square No. 4: Paint **Stonewedge Green**. Shade **Wedgewood Green**. Star is **Butter Yellow**.
5. Square No. 5: Paint **Wedgewood Green**. Shade **Forest Green**. X's are lined in pen, dots are **Dusty Mauve**, diagonal lines are **Blue Wisp**, straight lines are **Gypsy Rose**.
6. Square No. 6: Paint **Forest Green**. Paint heart **Blue Wisp**.
7. Square No. 7: Paint **Stonewedge Green**. Shade **Wedgewood Green**. Plaid lines are **Butter Yellow** and **Forest Green**.
8. Square No. 8: Paint **Wedgewood Green**. Paint every other mini square **Gypsy Rose**.

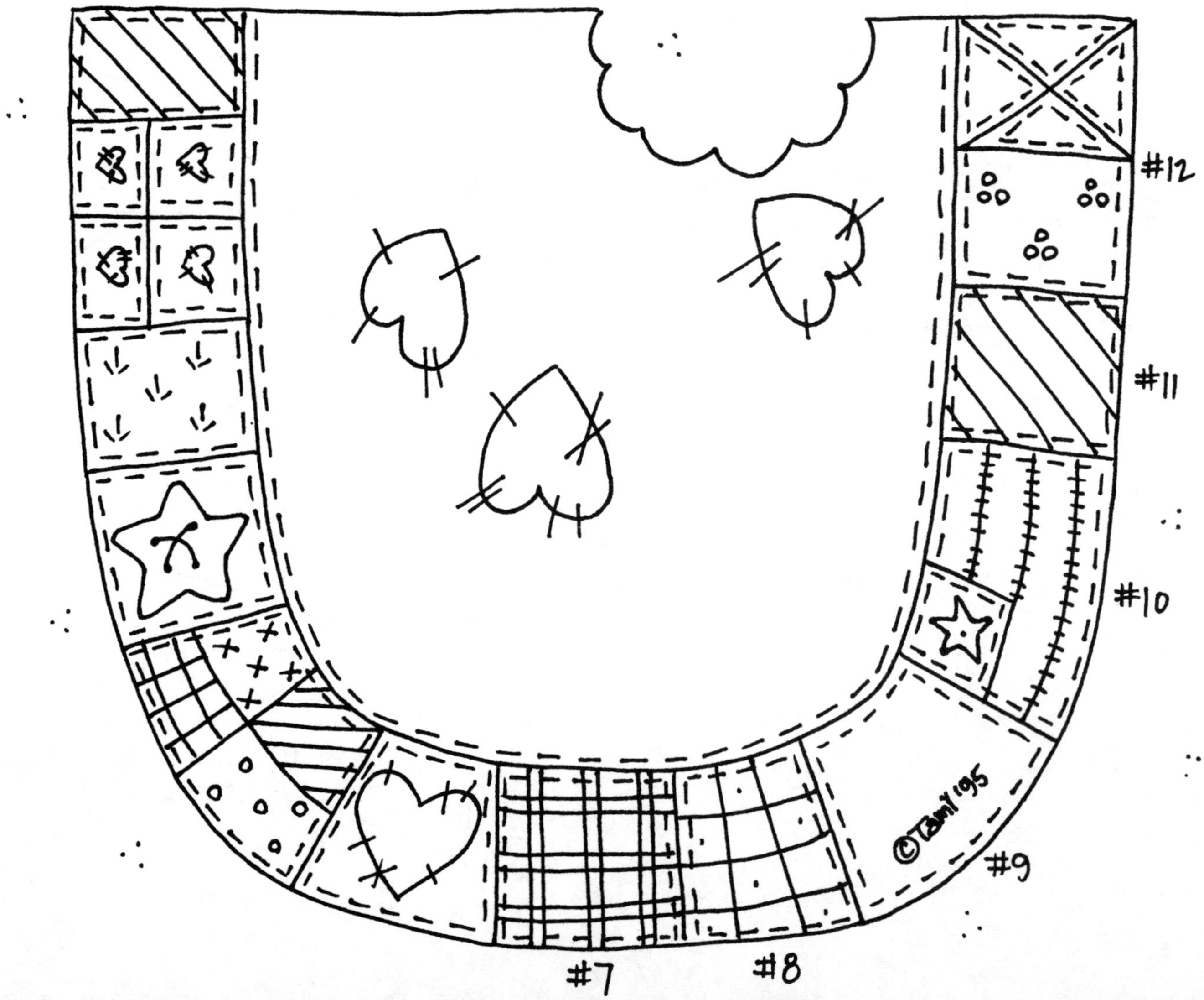

WATERMELON Cont.

9. Square No. 9: Paint **Village Green**, shade **Forest Green**.
10. Square No. 10: Paint **Forest Green**. Paint top and third stripes **Blue Wisp**. Star is **Butter Yellow**.
11. Square No. 11: Paint **Wedgewood Green**. Shade **Forest Green**, line **Dusty Mauve**.
12. Square No. 12: Paint **Stonewedge Green**. Shade **Wedgewood Green**. Paint two triangles **Forest Green**. Dots are **Butter Yellow**.
13. Black Lining Pen: Line/dot/stitch everything.
14. Spray with varnish.
15. Attach twisted wire to top corners to hang from Country Welcome Signs or Birdhouse Stand!

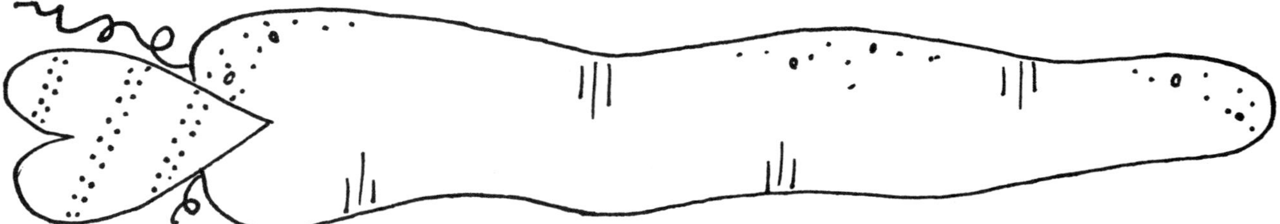

COUNTRY EASTER EGGS

PALETTE - Delta Ceramcoat

Light Ivory	Bambi Brown	Butter Yellow
Black	Gypsy Rose	Dusty Mauve
Wedgewood Green	Cape Cod	Forest Green

SUPPLIES
Mini Cow Bell
Jute
Spanish Moss
Wire or Hooks

1. Egg No. 1- Cow Egg: Paint entire egg **Light Ivory**. Stipple lightly **Bambi**. Shade egg **Bambi Brown**. Paint cow spots **Black**.
2. Egg No 2-Patches Egg: Paint entire egg **Gypsy Rose**. Stipple highlight **Light Ivory**. Shade **Dusty Mauve**. Lower patch is **Butter Yellow** with **Light Ivory** dots. Patch under heart is **Cape Cod** with **Light Ivory** pattern lines. Heart is **Light Ivory** with **Gypsy Rose** diagonal lines.
3. Egg No. 3-Watermelon Egg: Rind is **Forest Green**. Stipple highlights on rind and wavy line in **Wedgewood Green**. Watermelon is **Gypsy Rose**. Stipple highlight on watermelon in **Light Ivory**. Seeds and dots are **Black**.
4. Egg No. 4-Bunny Egg: Paint entire egg **Cape Cod**. Stipple highlight on egg in **Light Ivory**. Paint bunny **Light Ivory**. Stipple cheeks and line bow **Gypsy Rose**. Line face and do stitching in black lining pen
5. Egg No. 5-Crow Egg: Paint entire egg **Black**. Beak is **Butter Yellow**. Eyes are **Light Ivory**. Dot pupils **Black**.
6. Egg No. 6-Checkerboard Egg: Paint entire egg **Light Ivory**. Shade Bambi. Paint every other square **Gypsy Rose**.
7. Paint negative space **Bambi**.
8. Black Lining Pen: Line/stitch/dot everything.
9. Spray with varnish.
10. Glue Spanish Moss to bottom of eggs. Glue jute bow and mini cow bell to cow egg.
11. Attach hooks or wire to hang from one of the Country Welcome Signs or Birdhouse Stand during the Easter Bunny season!

COUNTRY EASTER EGGS

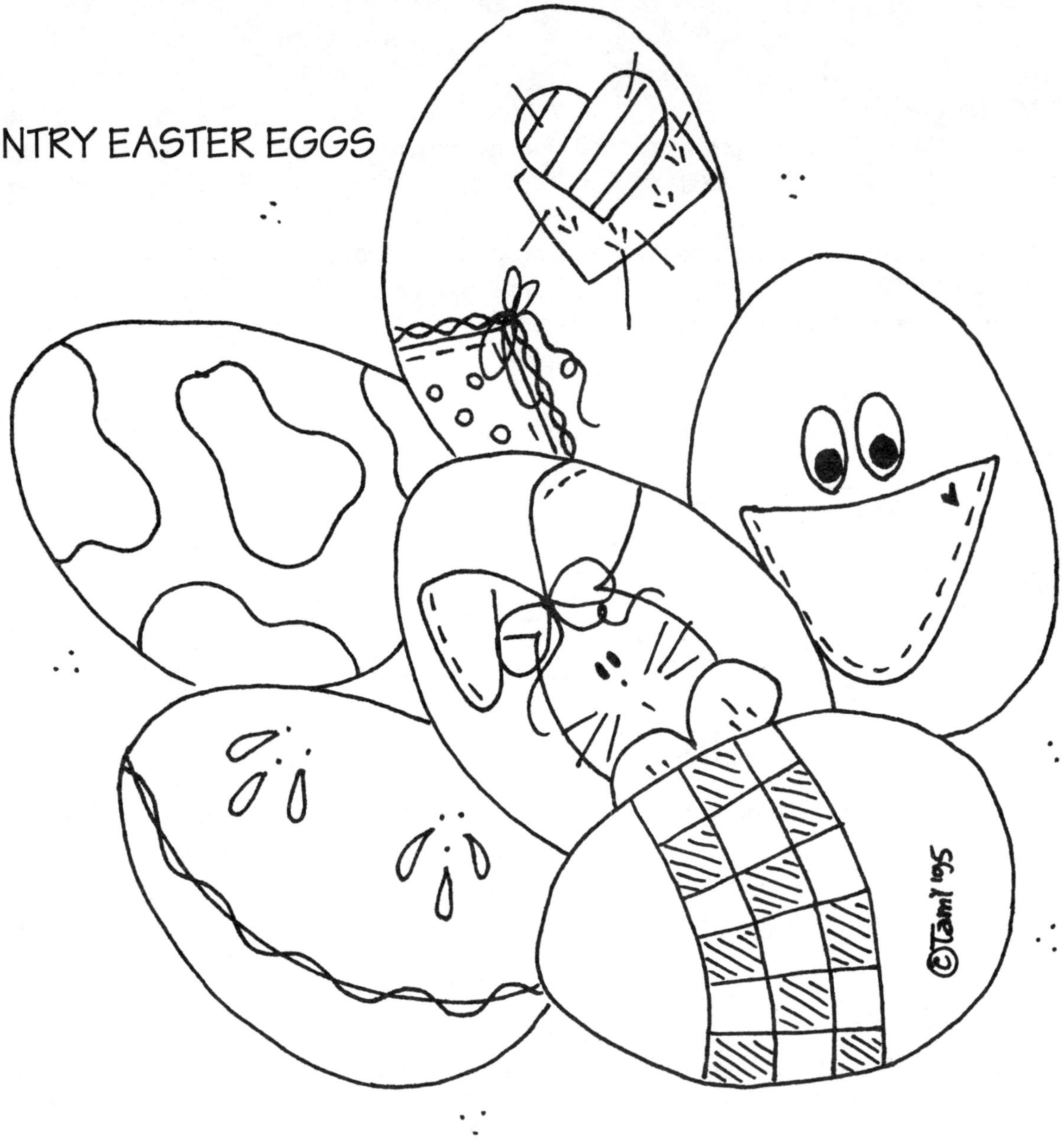

COUNTRY QUILT BLOCK

PALETTE - Delta Ceramcoat

Rose Mist	Cape Cod	Light Ivory
Rose Cloud	Sachet Pink	Taupe
Lavender Lace	Tide Pool Blue	Nightfall
Bouquet Pink	Wedgewood Green	

MISCELLANEOUS SUPPLIES

Buttons (Optional)
Wire or Hooks

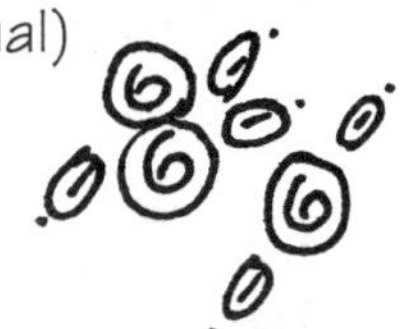

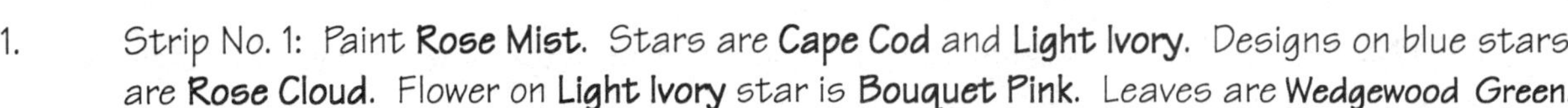

1. Strip No. 1: Paint **Rose Mist.** Stars are **Cape Cod** and **Light Ivory.** Designs on blue stars are **Rose Cloud.** Flower on **Light Ivory** star is **Bouquet Pink.** Leaves are **Wedgewood Green.**

2. Strip No. 2: Paint **Bouquet Pink.** Shade around all outside edges of strip using **Rose Mist.** Dots are **Rose Cloud, Rose Mist** and **Cape Cod.**

3. Strip No. 3: Paint **Sachet Pink.** Shade around all outside edges of strip using **Bouquet Pink.** Design lines are **Nightfall.**

4. Strip No. 4: Paint **Rose Cloud.** Shade around outside edges with **Sachet Pink.** Line **Rose Mist.**

5. Strip No. 5 (or center square): Paint **Taupe.** Shade lightly around all outside edges of square using **Cape Cod.**

6. Strip No. 6: Paint **Lavender Lace.** Shade around all outside edges of strip using **Tide Pool Blue.** Lines are **Light Ivory** and **Rose Cloud.**

COUNTRY QUILT BLOCK *Cont.*

7.   Strip No. 7: Paint **Tide Pool Blue**. Shade around all outside edges of strip using **Cape Cod**. Dots are **Rose Cloud**.

8.   Strip No. 8: Paint **Cape Cod**. Shade around all outside edges with **Nightfall**. Hearts are **Light Ivory** and **Sachet Pink**. Lines are **Nightfall**.

9.   Strip No. 9: Paint **Nightfall**. Lines are **Wedgewood Green**. Where lines intersect, paint squares **Rose Cloud**.

10.   Heart: Paint heart **Light Ivory**. Shade lightly **Cape Cod**. Flowers are **Rose Mist** and **Sachet Pink**. Leaves are **Wedgewood Green**.

11.   Patch: Paint patch **Rose Cloud**.

12.   Glue heart to center square.

13.   Black Lining Pen: Line/stitch everything.

14.   Splatter light with **Light Ivory**.

15.   Spray with vanish.

16.   Glue on buttons (optional). Attach hooks or twisted wire to hang from one of the Country Welcome Signs or Birdhouse Stand.

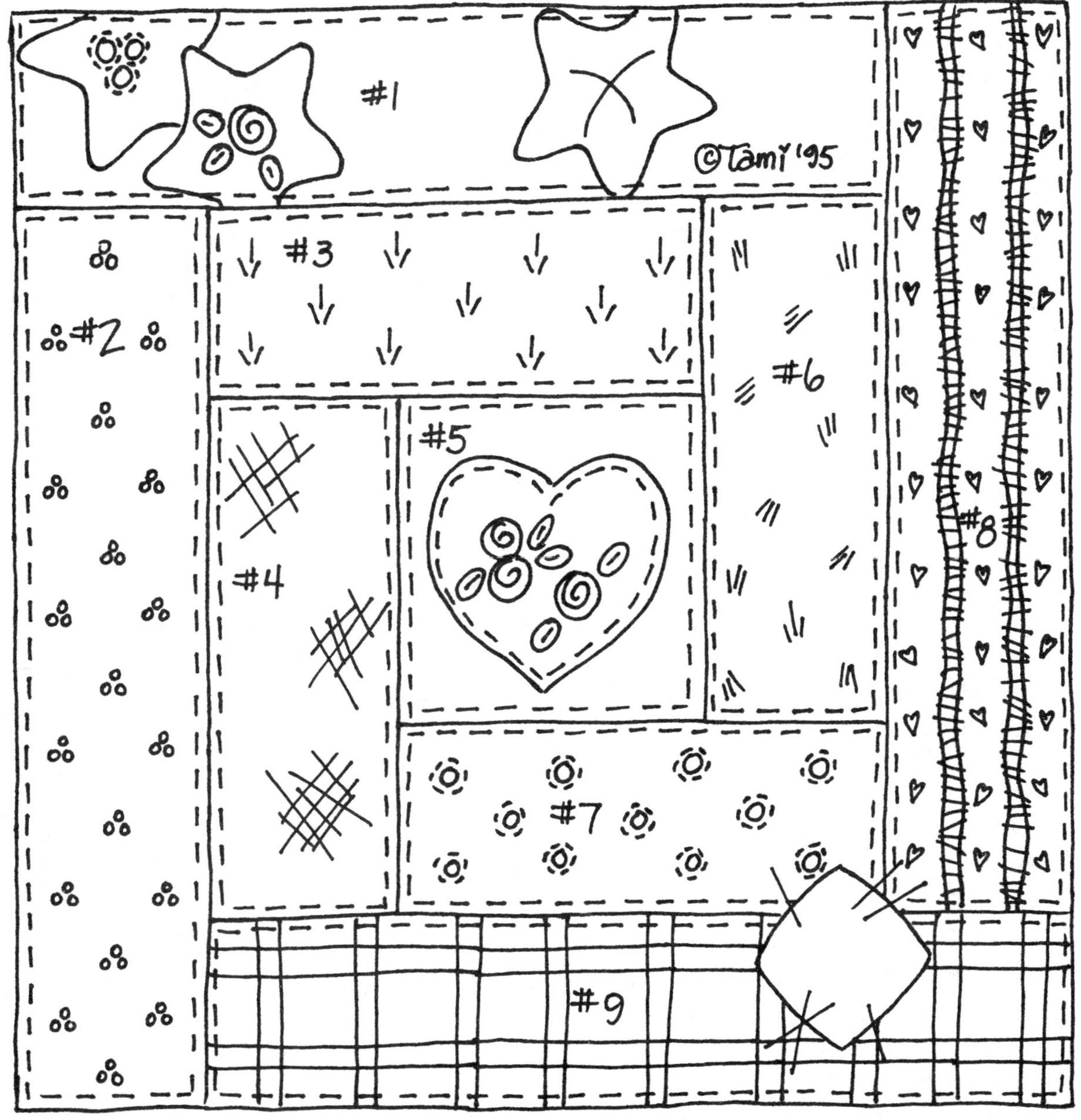

COUNTRY TULIPS

PALETTE-Delta Ceramcoat

Cactus Green

Bambi Brown

Antique Rose

Pale Yellow

Green Sea

Cape Cod

Butter Yellow

Lavender Lace

Sachet Pink

Light Ivory

MISCELLANEOUS SUPPLIES

Wire or Hooks

Fabric Scraps

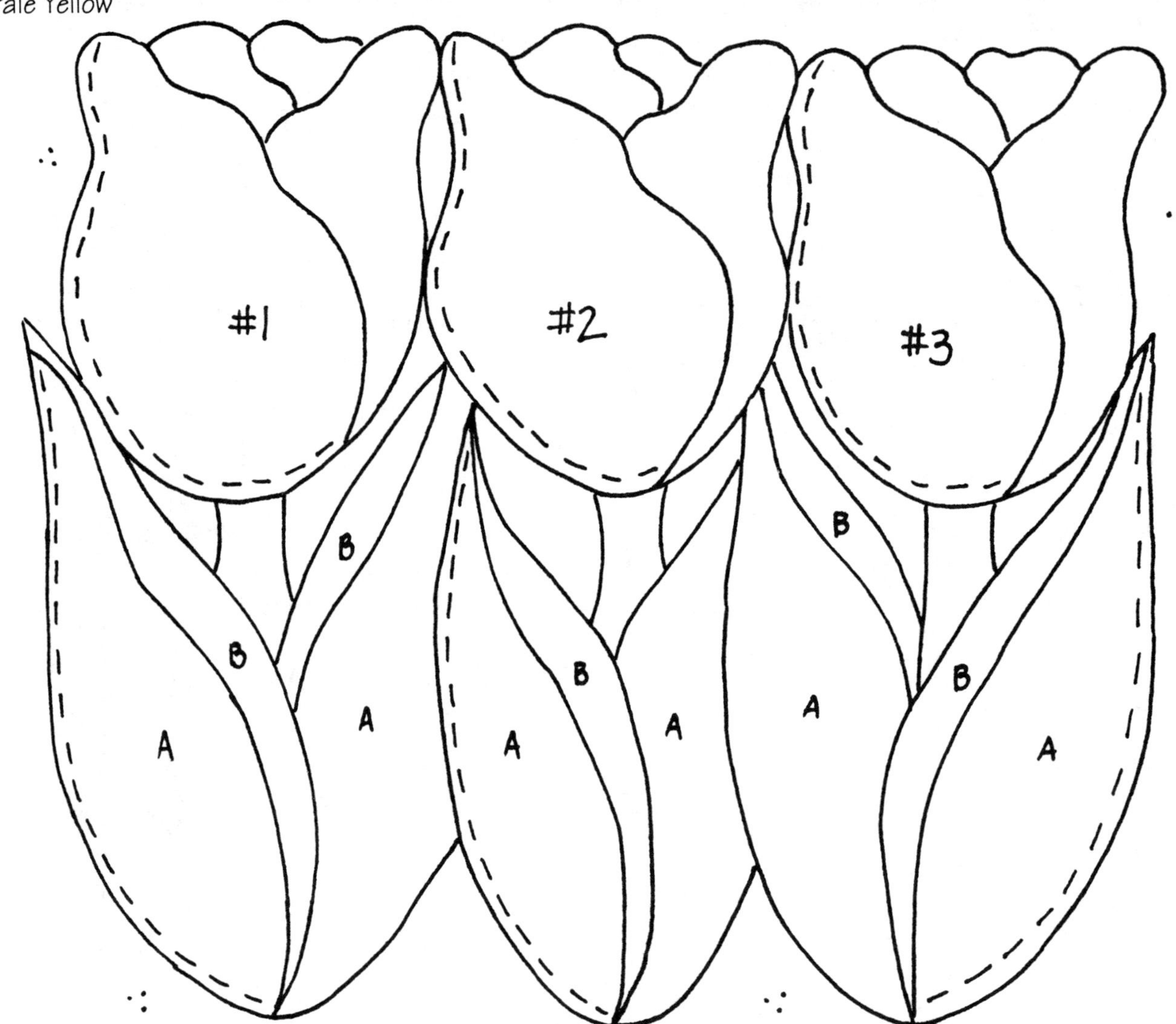

1. **Cactus Green:** Paint all "A" sections of leaves. Paint stems on Tulip No. 1 and No. 3.
2. **Green Sea:** Paint all "B" sections of leaves. Paint stem on tulip No. 2.
3. **Lavender Lace:** Paint tulip No. 1.
4. **Sachet Pink:** Paint Tulip No. 2.
5. **Pale Yellow:** Paint tulip No. 3.
6. **Cape Cod:** Shade tulip No. 1. Paint inside of tulip (at the top).
7. **Antique Rose:** Shade tulip No. 2. Paint inside of tulip (at the top).
8. **Butter Yellow:** Shade tulip No. 3. Paint inside of tulip (at the top).
9. **Green Sea:** Shade all leaves. Shade the stems on tulips No. 1 and No. 3.
10. **Bambi Brown:** Paint the negative spaces.
11. **Light Ivory:** Highlight leaves, stems, and tulips. Splatter everything.
12. **Black Lining Pen:** Line/stitch everything.
13. Spray with finishing spray/varnish.
14. Glue on buttons (optional) and fabric bows.
15. Attach wire or hooks to hang from one of the Country Welcome Signs or Birdhouse Stand.

HERE'S MY HEART

Valentine's Day wouldn't be complete without giving away your heart!

PALETTE - Delta Ceramcoat

Light Ivory	Bambi Brown
Antique Rose	Green Sea
Dusty Mauve	Candy Bar Brown

SUPPLIES

Buttons (Optional)
Wire or Hooks

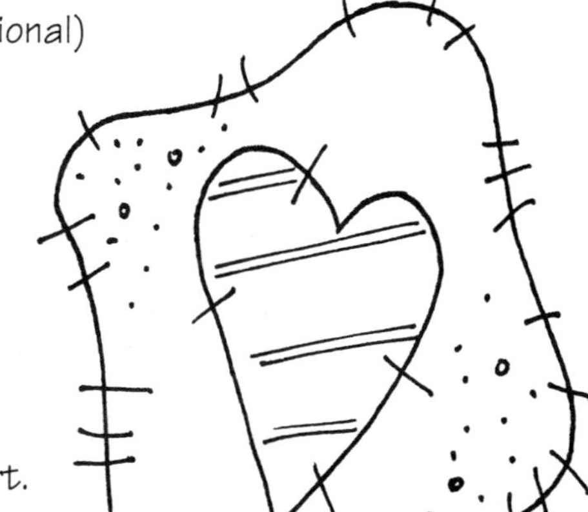

1. **Light Ivory:** Paint entire piece.
2. **Dusty Mauve:** Paint heart.
3. **Bambi Brown:** Shade bow.
4. **Candy Bar Brown:** Shade heart around the outside edges.
5. **Antique Rose:** Stipple highlight on heart.
6. **Light Ivory:** Strength the highlight by stippling again lightly on heart.
7. **Green Sea** and **Antique Rose:** Line plaid design on bow.
8. **Light Ivory:** Line "Here's My" and paint heart beside letters.
9. Black Lining Pen: Line bow and stitch around heart.
10. Spray with varnish.
11. Glue on buttons.
12. Attach wire or hooks to hang from one of the Country Welcome Signs or Birdhouse Stand!

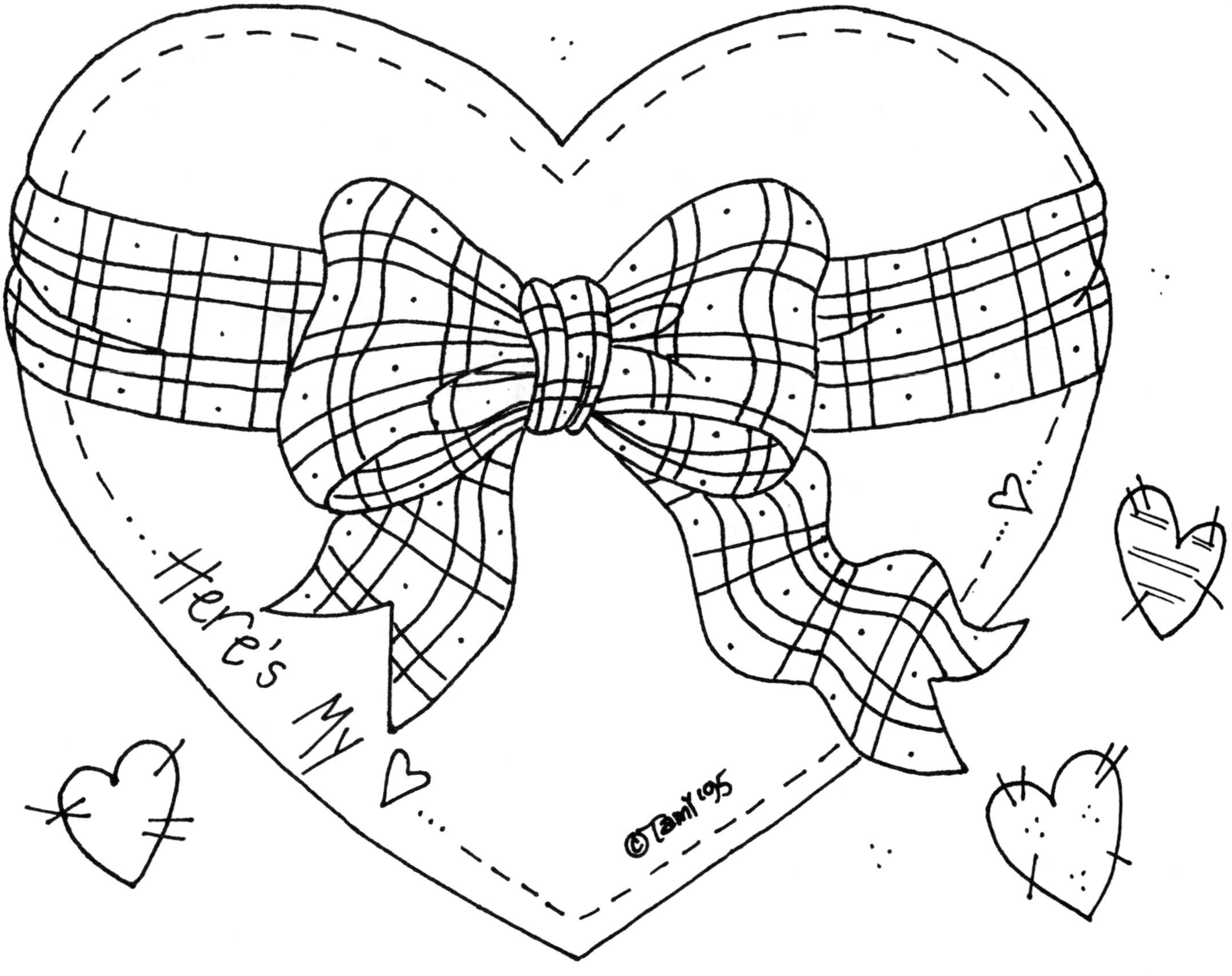

SPRING BUNNY WITH BABIES

PALETTE - Delta Ceramcoat

AC Flesh	Light Ivory	Wedgewood Green	Stonewedge Green
Bambi	White	Caucasion Flesh	Forest Green
Straw	Island Coral	Crocus Yellow	Bouquet Pink
White	Burgundy Rose		

MISCELLANEOUS SUPPLIES

Six Inch Battenburg Lace Doily, Tea Dyed   Spanish Moss

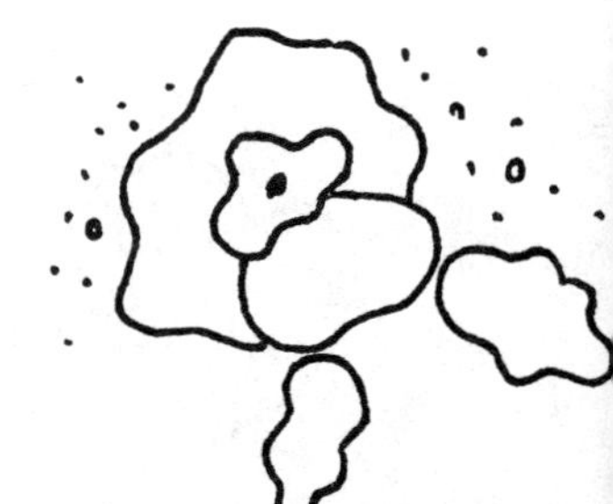

Note on Wood: I like 1/2 inch Birch wood for projects of this size. The baby bunnies and carrot are 1/4 inch thick and the base piece is six inches of 2 x 4 wood.

1.   **AC Flesh:** Paint Mama Bunny's face, hands, ears and legs. Paint baby bunnies entirely. (Don't worry about painting a lot of coats on these. We will be stippling over this to give a "bunny fur" look so the basecoat doesn't have to be real even).
2.   **Light Ivory:** Paint petticoat, front only.
3.   **Wedgewood Green:** Paint dress (front and entire back of dress and petticoat area).
4.   **Stonewedge Green:** Paint the back support piece.
5.   **Light Ivory** and **Stonewedge Green:** Mix equal parts of each. Paint grass area (don't forget the tiny patch between her knees) and carrot tops. Paint the back from the hem line on her dress down to edge of wood.
6.   **Straw:** Paint Mama bunny's sunbonnet (front and back).
7.   Painting the yellow pansies on her dress and in the grass: Main color is **Crocus Yellow**. Accent color is **Dusty Purple**. Center is **Vintage Wine**. Dot is **Light Ivory**.
8.   Painting the purple pansies on her dress and in the grass: Main color is **Dusty Purple**. Accent color is **Crocus Yellow**. Center is **Vintage Wine** with a **Light Ivory** dot.
9.   **Island Coral:** Paint carrot.
10.   **Caucasian Flesh:** Shade the left side of carrot.
11.   **Bambi Brown:** Shade fur (bottom of ears, sides of face, edges of hands, legs, etc.) Shade Mama bunny's sunbonnet on outside edges, brim (front and back), and a few long strokes in the middle.
12.   **Light Ivory:** Lightly stipple highlights on top and on the brim of sunbonnet.
13.   **White:** Stipple all three bunny's fur (ears, faces, hands and legs). Do sides and back, too, of Mama bunny.
14.   **Black:** Paint the bunny's eyes. Line Mama bunny's lashes.
15.   **Bouquet Pink:** Stipple cheeks and inside all bunny's ears. Paint noses and small hearts on Mama bunny's cheek.
16.   **Burgundy Rose:** Lightly deepen shade of cheeks and bottom of the ears.
17.   **Forest Green:** Shade dress (across bottom, on sleeve, sides of dress). Shade carrot top on left side and paint all leaves. Line the stems.
18.   **AC Flesh:** Shade bottom of petticoat.
19.   **Burgundy Rose:** Line plaid design on petticoat.
20.   **Stonewedge Green:** Shade grass next to feet and by the cut edge of wood.
21.   **White:** Lightly stipple here and there on dress. Highlight eyes and nose.
22.   **Forest Green:** Do "three dot" design in grass.
23.   **AC Flesh:** Do "three dot" design on dress.

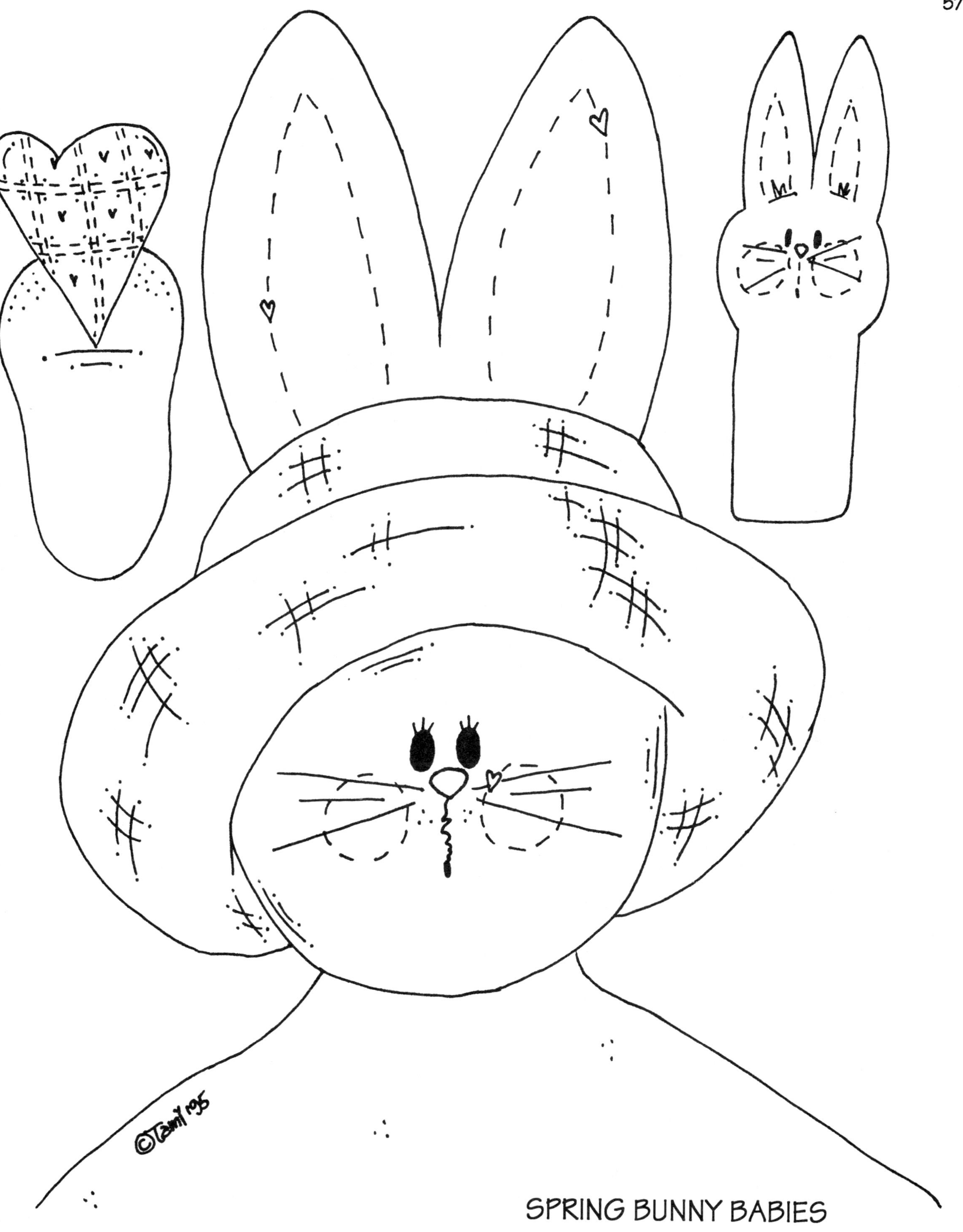

SPRING BUNNY BABIES

SPRING BUNNY BABIES

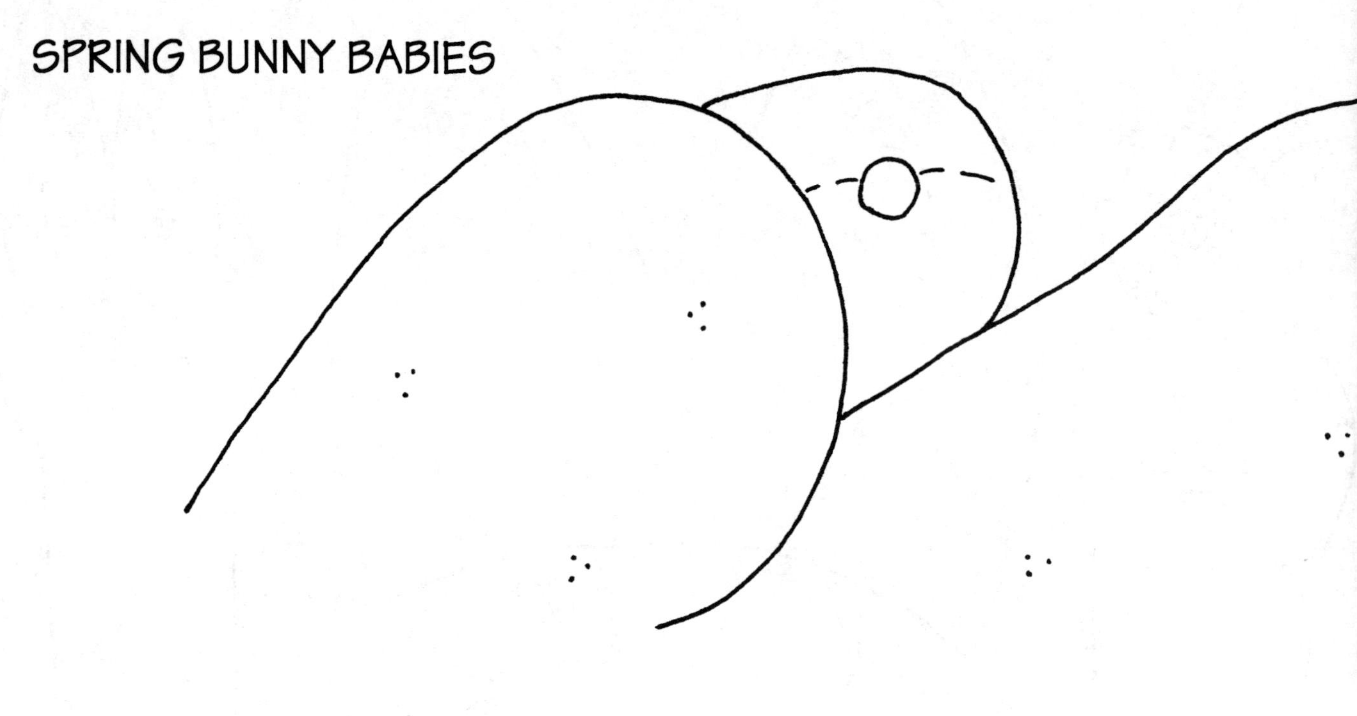

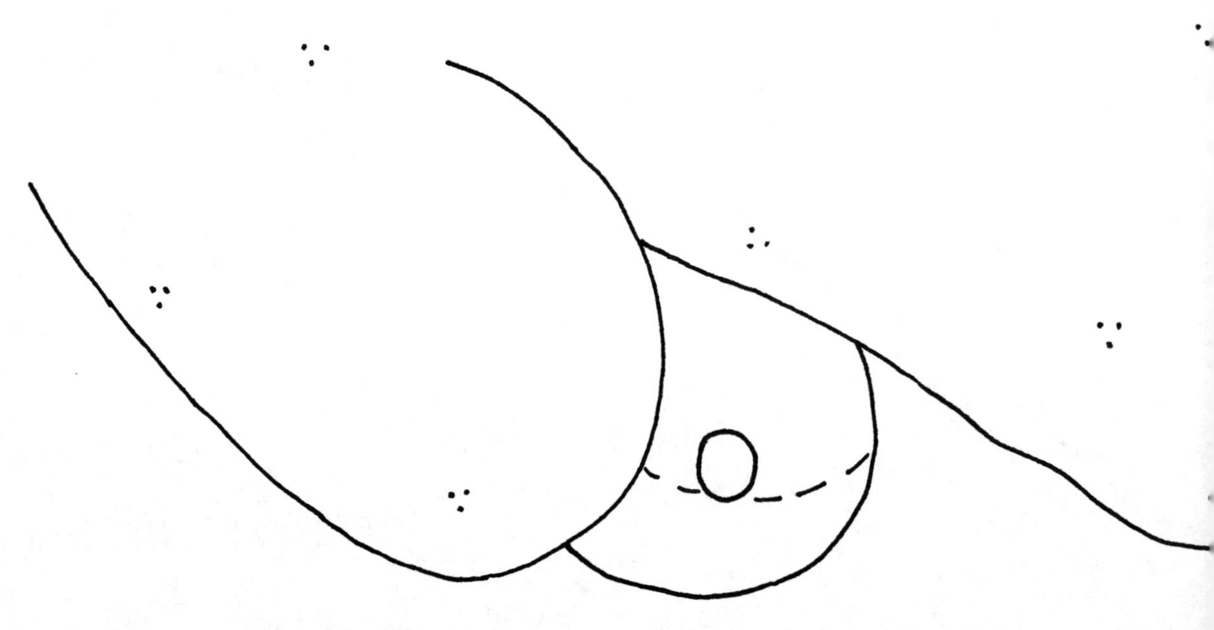

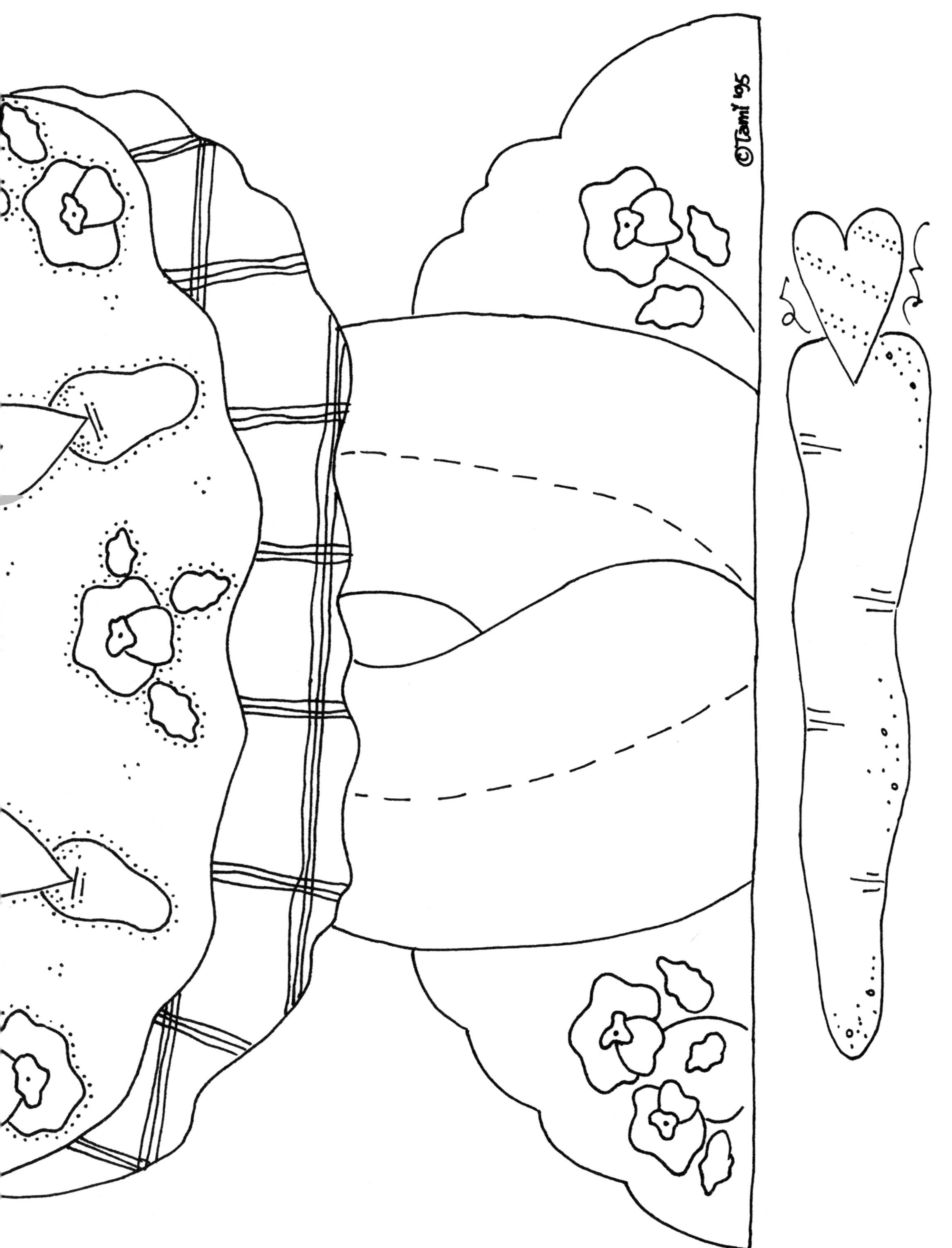

SPRING BUNNY BABIES Continued

24.   Black Lining Pen: Line/stitch everything. Line the faces, stitching, outlines and dots around pansies and carrot. NOTE: Dot around pansies and leaves in the grass the same as on dress. Draw small hearts on the carrot top.

25.   Spray with varnish.

26.   Paint pansy design on collar using one of the pansy designs on dress. Lay doily over design and trace on lightly. Paint following pansy on dress instructions.

27.   Glue on fabric bow (1" x 12") on Mama bunny's hat brim. Make two knots of fabric (1" x 4") and glue to each foot. After putting fabric (5" x 14") through holes in hands, glue in place on back. Glue bottom edge to dress, tucking under edge of fabric. Glue small knots of fabric on the babies. Glue carrot and babies in place. Glue tufts of Spanish Moss around them. Glue the back support piece on about 1/2 inch from bottom. You could glue on a large pom-pom in back for Mama bunny's tail if you'd like! Cut doily carefully and glue in place for collar.

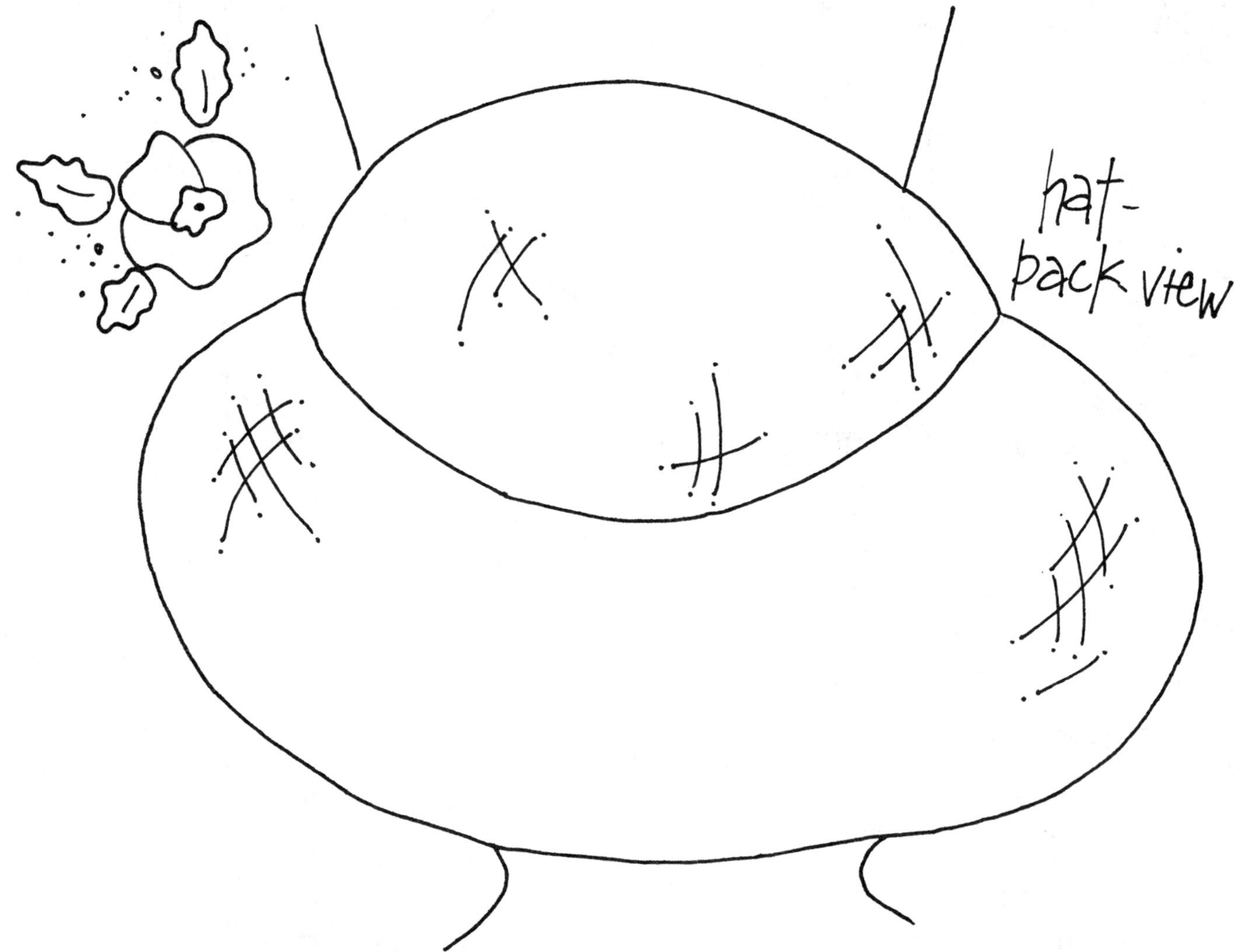

SPRING BUNNY BABIES

We paint, then touch it up, then touch-up our touch-up...don't we? Remember...the sign of a true artist is knowing when to quit!

SUMMER FLOWERS

PALETTE - Delta Ceramcoat

Butter Yellow	Territorial Beige	Burnt Umber	Light Ivory
Wedgewood Green	Forest Green	Empire Gold	

MISCELLANEOUS SUPPLIES

Raffia	Hooks or Wire	Buttons

1. **Butter Yellow:** Paint entire piece.
2. **Territorial Beige:** Paint centers of flowers.
3. **Wedgewood Green:** Paint leaves.
4. **Empire Gold:** Shade flowers.
5. **Forest Green:** Shade leaves.
6. **Burnt Umber:** Shade centers of flowers.
7. **Light Ivory:** Lightly splatter.
8. Black Lining Pen: Line/stitch everything.
9. Glue on buttons, overlapping here and there for dimension. Glue on raffia bow.
10. Attach twisted wire or hooks to hang from one of the Country Welcome Signs or Birdhouse Stand!

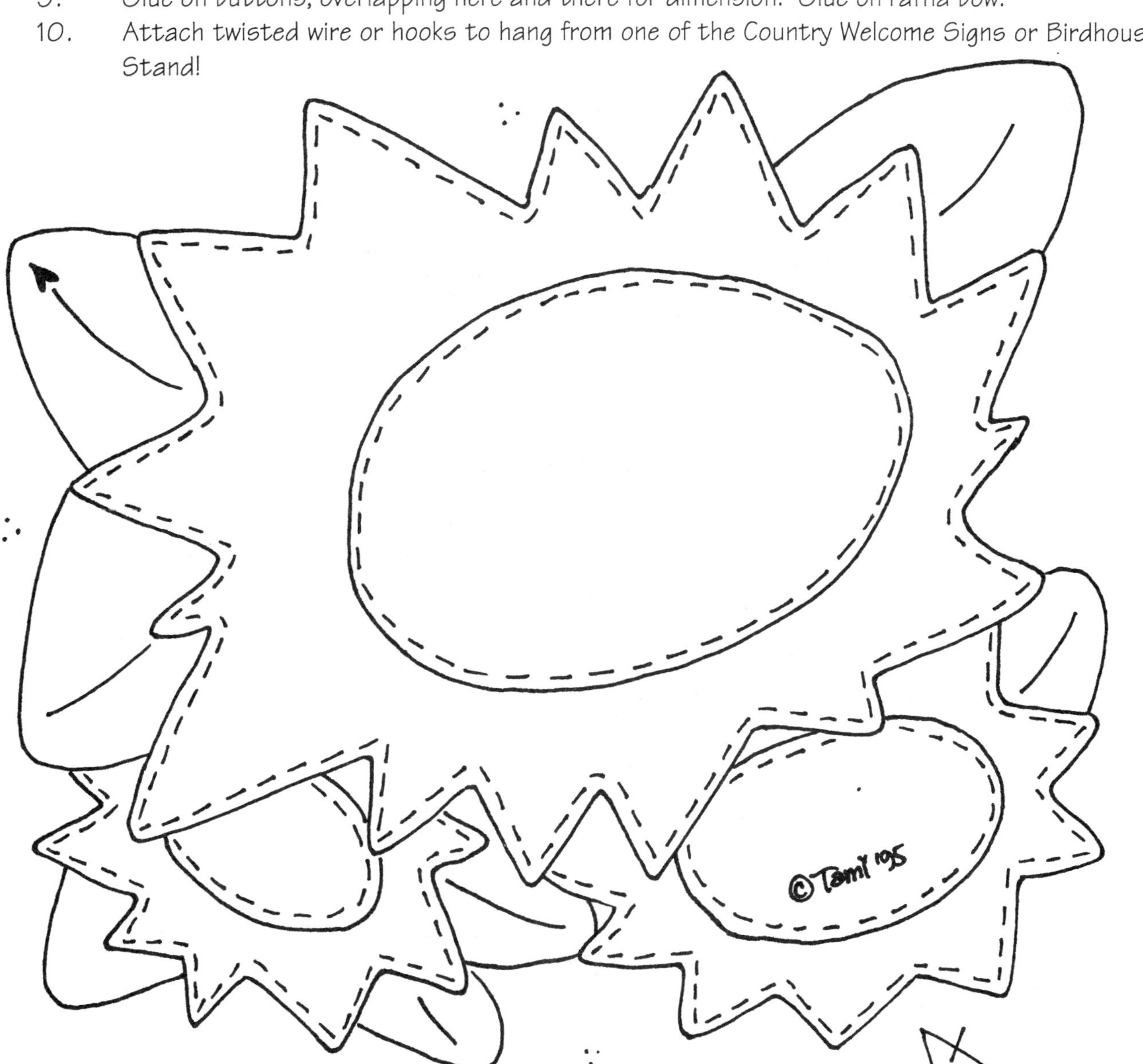

TEDDY BEAR POT

PALETTE-Delta Ceramcoat

Bouquet Pink	Sachet Pink	Light Ivory	Antique Rose
Bambi	Burnt Umber		

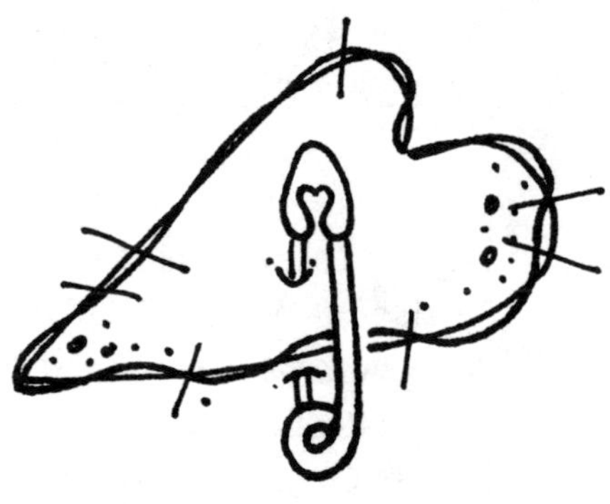

MISCELLANEOUS SUPPLIES: Six or Eight Inch Clay Pot

1. **Bouquet Pink:** Paint pot.
2. **Sachet Pink:** Paint blocks.
3. **Light Ivory:** Lightly splatter entire pot.
4. **Bambi:** Paint bear.
5. **Light Ivory:** Paint bear's bow.
6. **Sachet Pink:** Paint bear's heart.
7. Mix one drop **Bambi** and one drop **Light Ivory** together. Using this mixture, paint paws on bear's legs and muzzle. Line the "fuzzy" lines on bear's fur.
8. **Antique Rose:** Paint bear's nose and shade bow.
9. **Burnt Umber:** Shade bear.
10. **Light Ivory:** Paint lace.
11. **Antique Rose:** Shade lace.
12. **Bouquet Pink:** Paint comma stroke and dot pattern on lace.

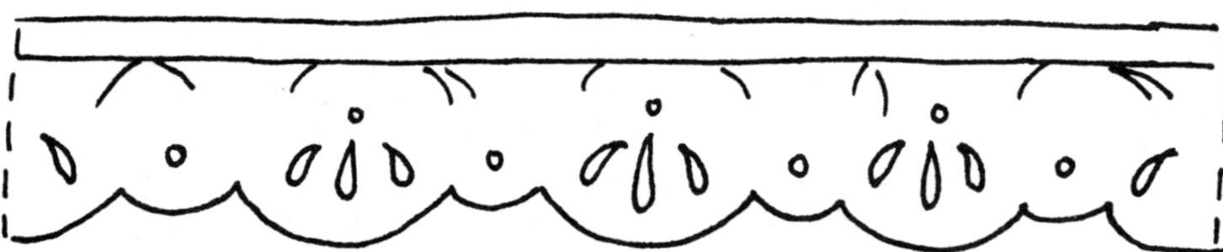

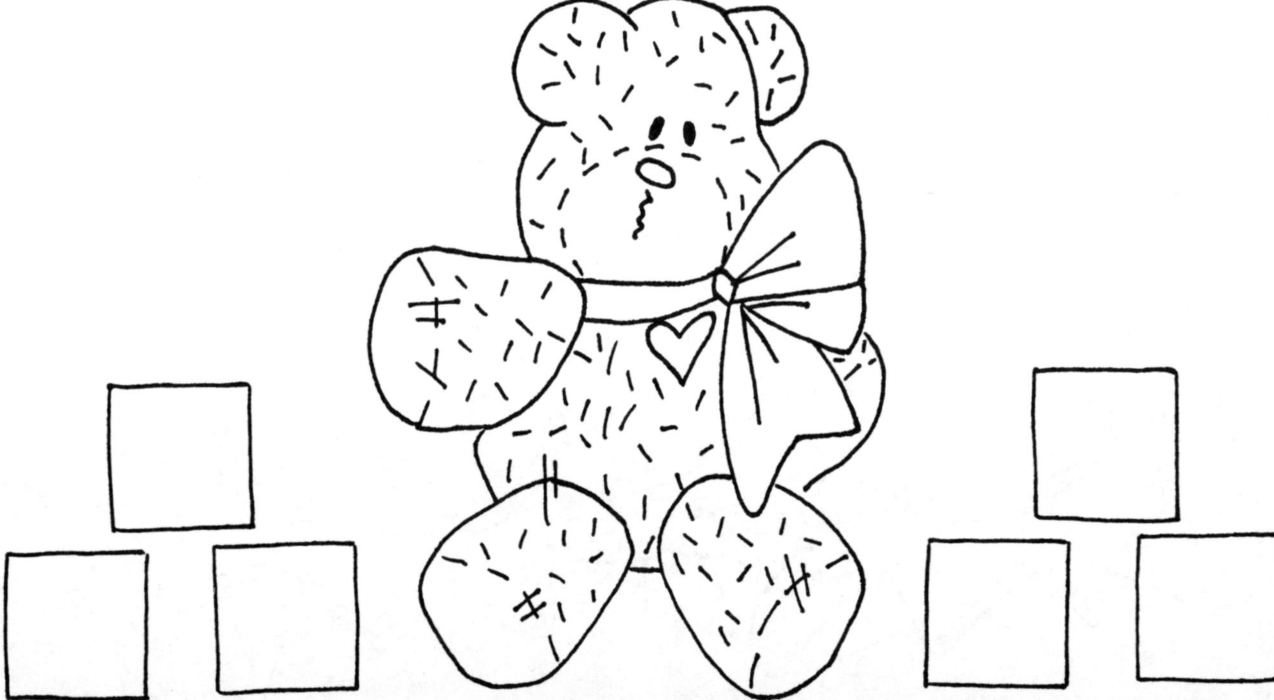

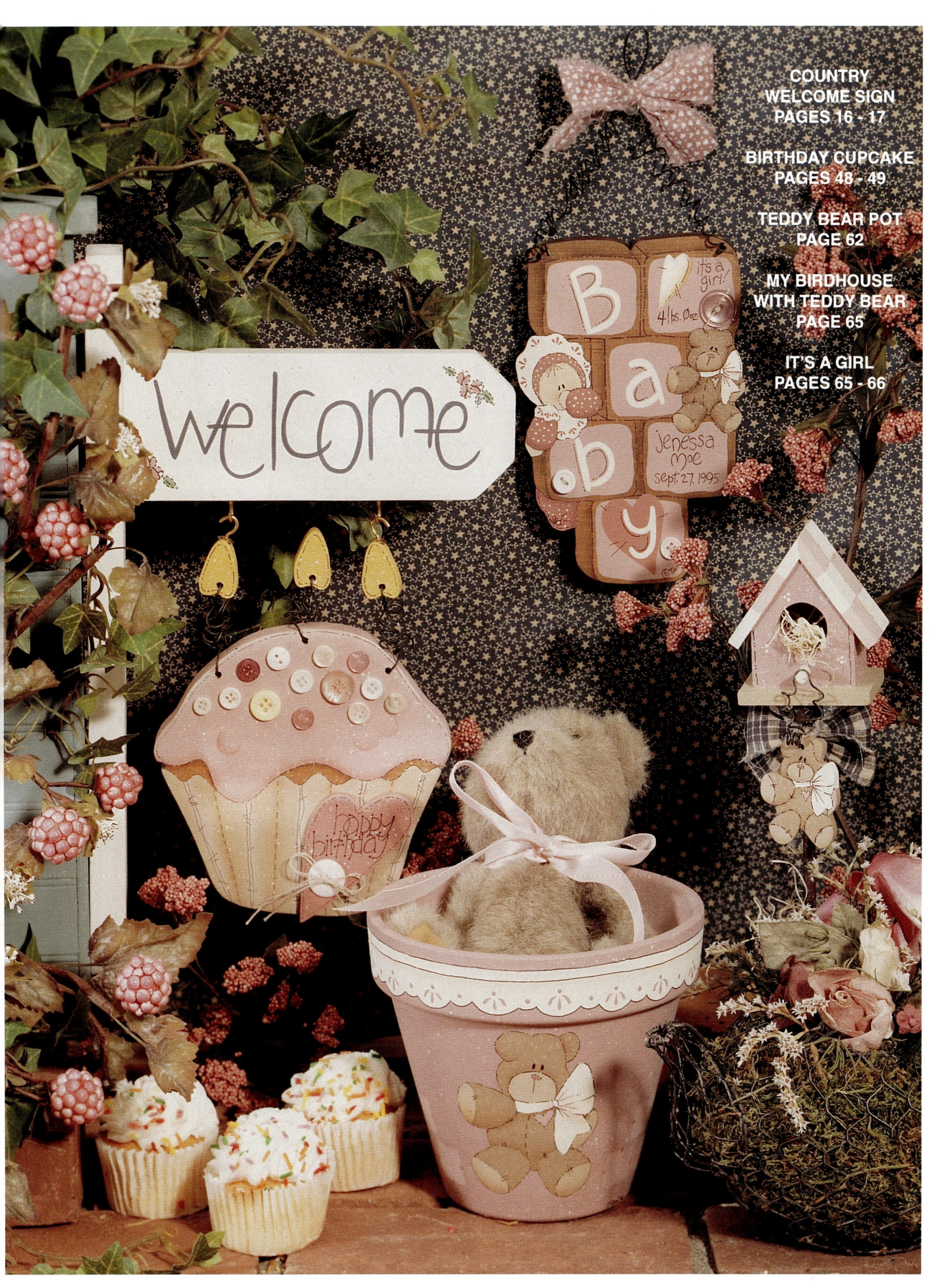

COUNTRY
WELCOME SIGN
PAGES 16 - 17

BIRTHDAY CUPCAKE
PAGES 48 - 49

TEDDY BEAR POT
PAGE 62

MY BIRDHOUSE
WITH TEDDY BEAR
PAGE 65

IT'S A GIRL
PAGES 65 - 66

Welcome

BABY

it's a girl!
4 lbs. 0 oz.
Jenessa Moe
Sept. 27, 1995

happy birthday

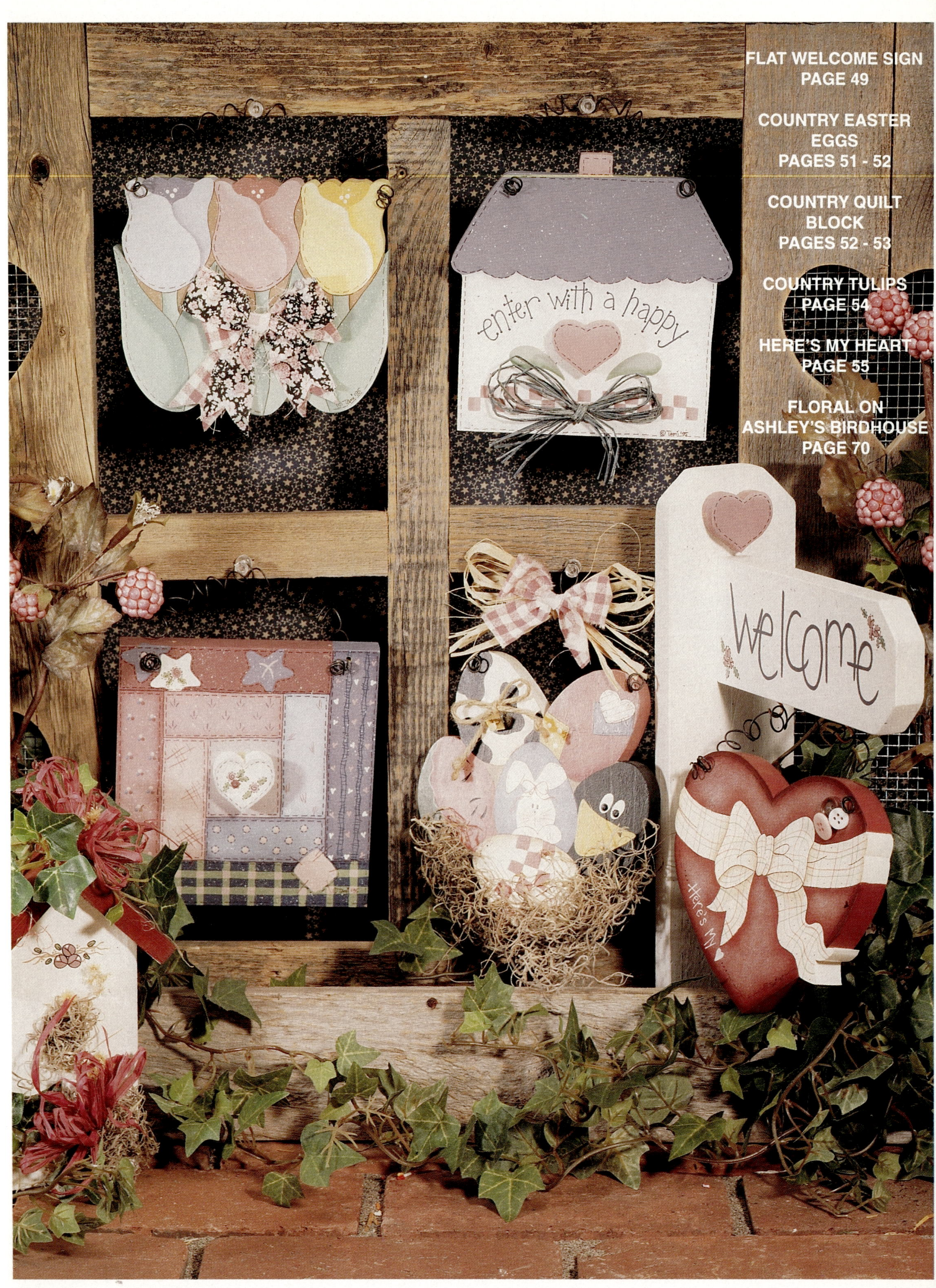
FLAT WELCOME SIGN
PAGE 49

COUNTRY EASTER
EGGS
PAGES 51 - 52

COUNTRY QUILT
BLOCK
PAGES 52 - 53

COUNTRY TULIPS
PAGE 54

HERE'S MY HEART
PAGE 55

FLORAL ON
ASHLEY'S BIRDHOUSE
PAGE 70

enter with a happy

welcome

Here's My

MINI BIRDHOUSE WITH TEDDY BEAR

PALETTE - Delta Ceramcoat

Bouquet Pink	Antique Rose	Burnt Umber	Sachet Pink
Light Ivory	Bambi		

Paint bear following instructions of "It's A Girl". Birdhouse is painted **Bouquet Pink**, with **Light Ivory** "Three Dot" design. Roof is **Light Ivory** and **Sachet Pink** checks. Heart on roof is **Light Ivory**. Base of birdhouse is **Bambi**. Dowel is **Burnt Umber**. Stand base piece is **Antique Rose**. Splatter entire piece **Light Ivory**, then splatter entire piece **Antique Rose**. Line/stitch everything. Spray finish piece with a finish spray or varnish. Glue natural excelsior to stand base piece and in hole of birdhouse. Wrap wire through top of bear and hang from perch. Glue fabric bow to dowel.

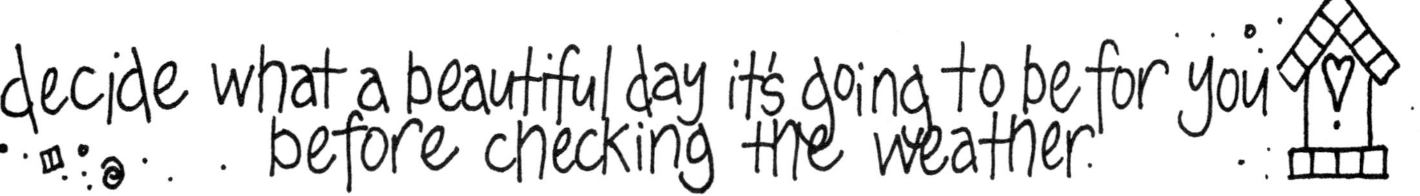

IT'S A GIRL!

This pattern is dedicated to Jenessa Angela Moe, niece and sweetheart... though miniature in size, she's stolen our hearts in a big way!

PALETTE- Delta Ceramcoat

Burnt Umber	Bambi Brown	Fleshtone	Light Ivory
Antique Rose	Sachet Pink	Rose Mist	

MISCELLANEOUS SUPPLIES

Buttons	Wire or hooks

1. **Burnt Umber:** Water paint down until it's real thin, making a wash. Paint whole piece.
2. **Bambi Brown:** Paint bear.
3. **Fleshtone:** Paint baby's face and hands.
4. **Light Ivory:** Paint baby's bib, top of sleeve, top of bonnet, bear's bow, and small heart.
5. **Antique Rose:** Paint baby's hat and clothes.
6. **Sachet Pink:** Paint front of blocks and heart on bear.
7. Mix one drop of **Bambi Brown** and one drop **Light Ivory** together. Using this mixture, paint paws on bear's legs and muzzle. Line the "fuzzy" lines on bear's fur.
8. **Antique Rose:** Paint large heart. Paint bear's nose. Shade bear's bow.
9. **Burnt Umber:** Shade blocks, bear and small heart.
10. **Rose Mist:** Shade baby's clothes. Paint design on baby's bonnet, sleeve and bib.
11. **Light Ivory:** Line letters b-a-b-y. Dot design on baby's clothes.
12. Black Lining Pen: Line/stitch everything.
13. Spray varnish.
14. Glue on buttons. Attach twisted wire or hooks to hang alone or on one of the Country Welcome Signs or Birdhouse Stand!

IT'S A GIRL!

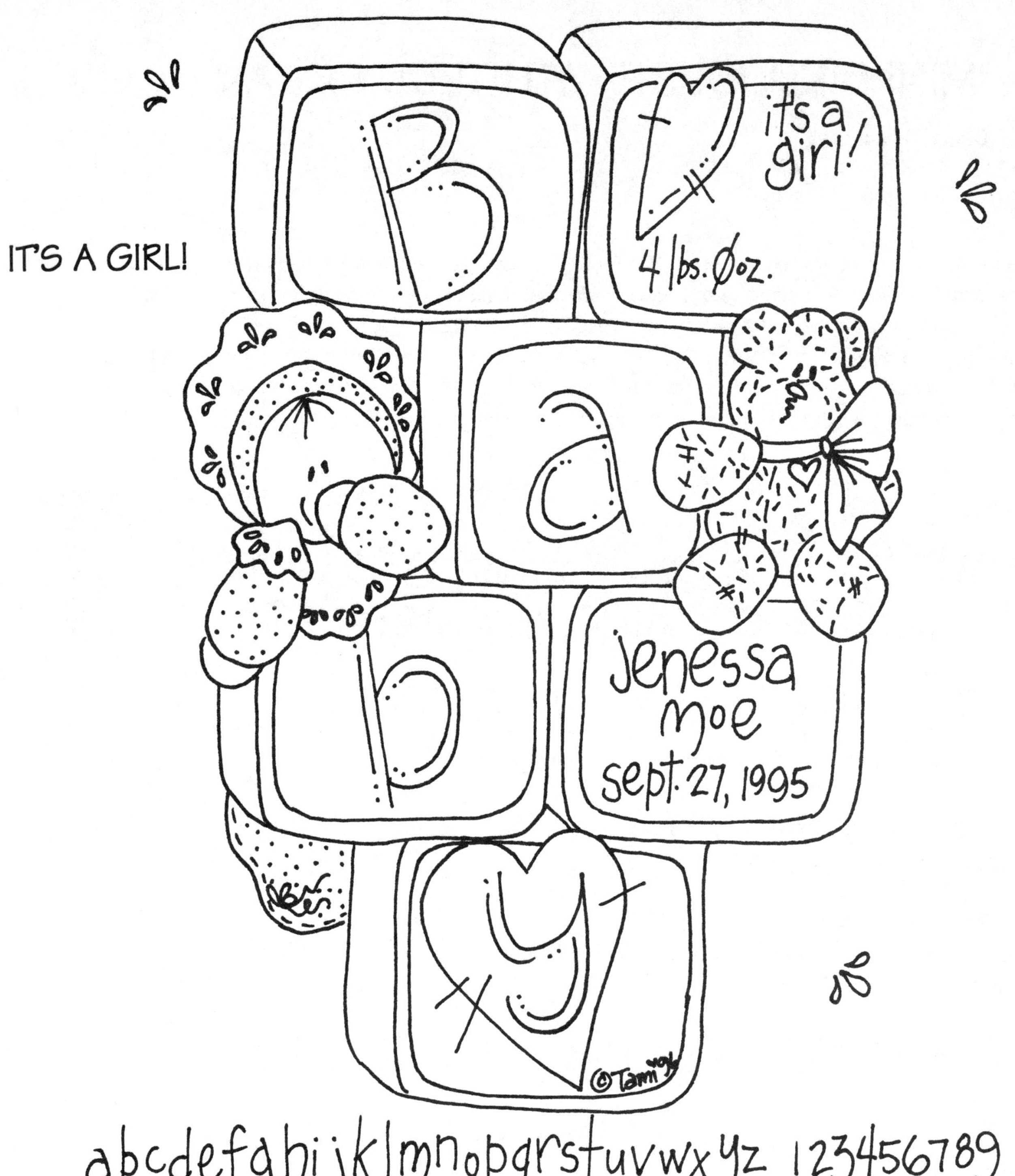

abcdefghijklmnopqrstuvwxyz 123456789

IT'S A BOY!

PALETTE - Delta Ceramcoat

Bambi Brown	Nightfall	Burgundy Rose	Butter Yellow
Cape Cod	Light Ivory		

MISCELLANEOUS SUPPLIES

Buttons	Thread	Wire or Hooks

1. **Light Ivory:** Paint entire piece.
2. **Bambi Brown:** Paint bear.
3. **Nightfall:** Paint boat and mast (pole).

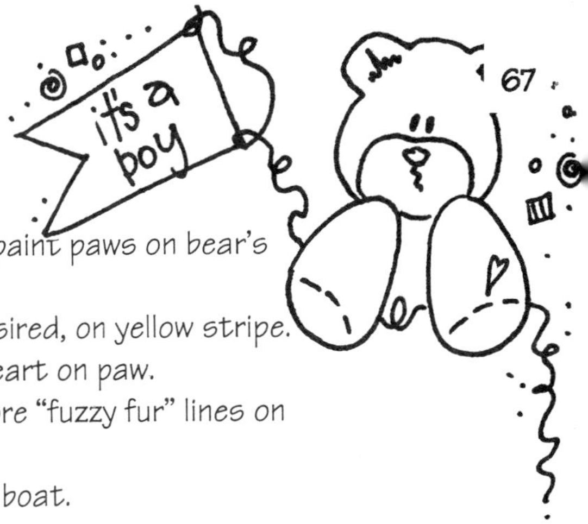

4. **Burgundy Rose:** Paint the right sail.
5. **Butter Yellow:** Paint the flag and the stripe on the right sail.
6. **Cape Cod:** Shade left sail.
7. **Bambi Brown:** Shade cloud, flag, and yellow stripe on sail.
8. Mix one drop **Bambi** and one drop **Light Ivory.** Using this mixture paint paws on bear's legs and muzzle. Line "fuzzy fur" on bear.
9. **Nightfall:** Line "It's A Boy!" on left sail. Individualize weight, if desired, on yellow stripe.
10. **Burgundy Rose:** Paint dots on left sail. Paint bear's nose and heart on paw.
11. **Light Ivory:** Lightly line design on mast (pole). Highlight a few more "fuzzy fur" lines on bear. Line name and date of birth on boat.
12. Using **Burgundy Rose, Butter Yellow** and **Cape Cod,** paint top of boat.
13. **Black Lining Pen:** Line/stitch everything. Line "ships ahoy" on flag.
14. **Light Ivory:** Lightly splatter.
15. Spray with varnish.
16. Glue on buttons. If desired, tie a knot of thread in a button or two.
17. Screw in hooks or wire to hang on your Country Welcome Sign or Birdhouse Stand!

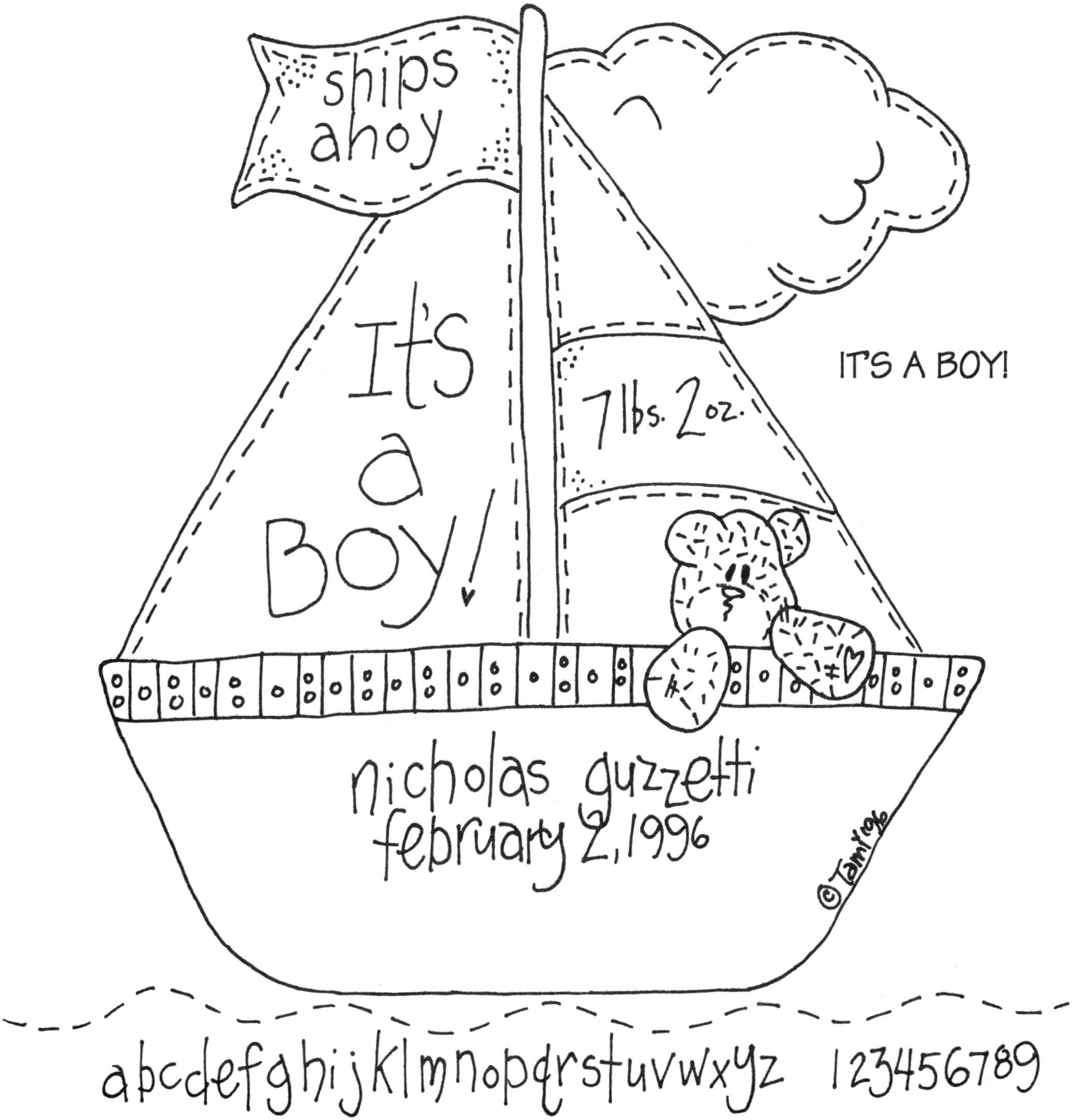

WATERING CAN

PALETTE- Delta Ceramcoat

Wedgewood Green	Caucasian Flesh	Forest Green	Cayenne
Butter Yellow	Light Ivory	Black Green	

MISCELLANEOUS SUPPLIES

Buttons (Optional)   Jute

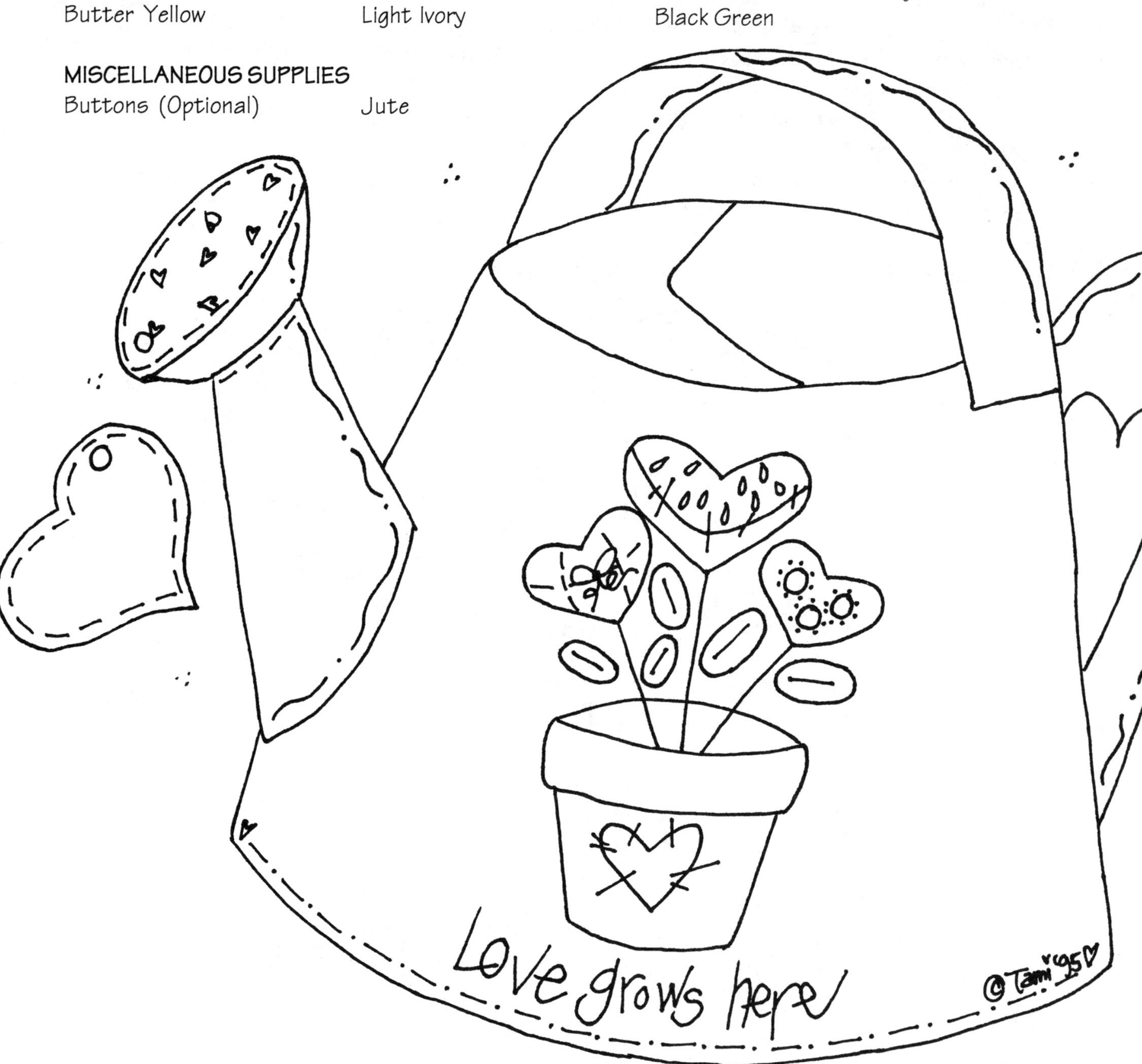

1.   **Wedgewood Green:** Paint entire can.
2.   **Caucasian Flesh:** Paint flower pot and top of watermelon (center) heart.
3.   **Forest Green:** Paint inside of can. Shade can. Paint leaves. Paint rind of watermelon heart.
4.   **Black Green:** Paint negative areas. Paint seeds on watermelon heart.
5.   **Butter Yellow:** Paint left heart.
6.   Paint right heart **Light Ivory**. Dot in **Butter Yellow**.
7.   Paint hanging heart **Light Ivory**. Lightly splatter **Forest Green**. Hearts are **Light Ivory**, **Butter Yellow** and **Caucasian Flesh**.
8.   **Cayenne:** Shade flower pot.

WATERING CAN Cont.

9. **Butter Yellow:** Paint heart on pot.
10. **Light Ivory:** Lightly stipple all over (except negative areas and inside can) to highlight.
11. **Black Green:** Line letters "love grows here". (Remember that thinning your paint with a little water will make it easier to have smooth thin lines).
12. Black Lining Pen: Line/stitch everything.
13. Spray with finishing spray/varnish.
14. Glue on buttons (optional).
15. Attach twisted wire or hooks for use on the Country Welcome Sign or Birdhouse Stand!

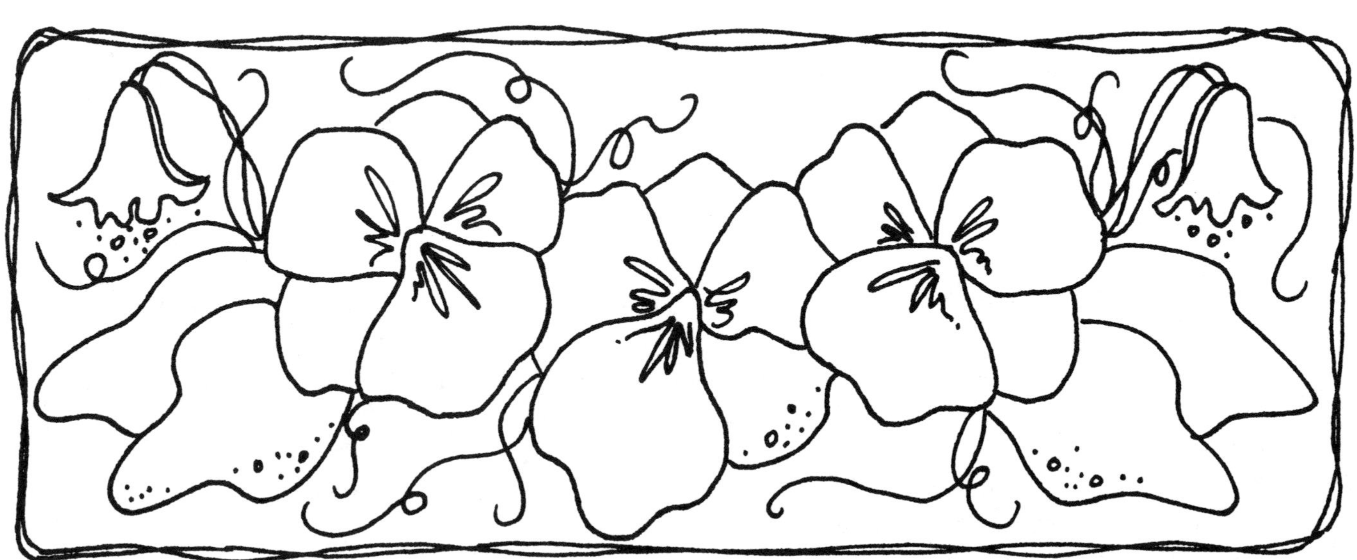

PANSY PIN

PALETTE-Delta Ceramcoat

Wedgewood Green	Forest Green	Wisteria
Dusty Purple	Light Chocolate	Light Ivory

MISCELLANEOUS SUPPLIES

Two inch heart-shaped Battenburg Lace Doily, tea dyed
Fabric Strips   Button

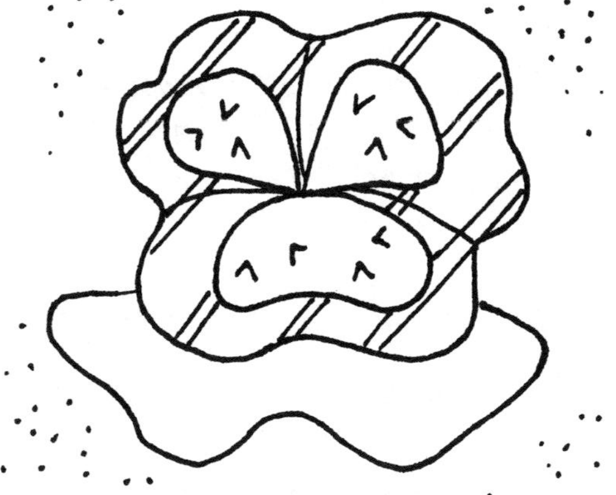

1. **Wedgewood Green:** Paint leaves.
2. **Forest Green:** Shade leaves.
3. **Wisteria:** Paint pansy.
4. **Light Ivory:** Paint accent areas on pansy.
5. **Dusty Purple:** Shade pansy.
6. **Light Chocolate:** Shade the outside of the **Light Ivory** areas.
7. **Dusty Purple:** Shade the inside of the **Light Ivory** areas.
8. **Light Chocolate:** Line plaid lines on pansy.
9. **Wedgewood Green:** Line design in **Light Ivory** area.
10. Black Lining Pen: Line/stitch everything.
11. Tie heavy thread in button. Glue button to center of pansy. Tie fabric strip 3/4" x 12" long into bow. Glue fabric bow to doily just under wood piece. Glue pin to back.

POTTED PANSIES

I'd like to dedicate this pattern to my daughter, Angela, who willingly spent hours in the office so I could be in the painting studio creating instead of working! Thanks, Angie-pansie!

PALETTE- Delta Ceramcoat

Caucasian Flesh	Cayenne
Crocus Yellow	Empire Gold
Vintage Wine	Dusty Purple
Light Ivory	Light Chocolate

MISCELLANEOUS SUPPLIES

Fabric Scraps	Spanish Moss

1. **Caucasian Flesh:** Paint pot.
2. **Cayenne:** Shade pot (under lip of pot and outside edges).
3. Painting pansy No. 3: Main color is **Crocus Yellow.** Shade **Empire Gold.** Accent color is **Caucasian Flesh.** Shade **Vintage Wine.** Center is **Vintage Wine.**
4. Painting Pansy No. 1 and No. 2: Main color is **Dusty Purple.** Shade **Vintage Wine.** Accent color is **Crocus Yellow.** Shade **Vintage Wine.** Center is **Vintage Wine.**
5. **Light Ivory:** Stipple highlight on pot. Dot centers of flowers. Paint bow on pot.
6. **Light Chocolate:** Shade bow.
7. Black Lining Pen: Line/stitch/dot everything.
8. Paint dowel stems **Wedgewood Green.**
9. Glue in place. Tie fabric strips for leaves. Glue in Spanish Moss.

FLORAL ON ASHLEY'S BIRDHOUSE

My daughter, Ashley, made this birdhouse for me for Mother's Day. She let me paint a small floral swag on it and said I could share it with you!

PALETTE-Delta Ceramcoat

Bouquet Pink	Bambi Brown	Wedgewood Green	Light Ivory

1. **Bouquet Pink:** Dot flowers.
2. **Wedgewood Green:** Paint leaves.
3. **Light Ivory:** Dot highlights on flowers.
4. **Bambi Brown:** Line sticks and three dot pattern.
5. Black Lining Pen: Line.

Susan Scheewe Publications Inc.

13435 N.E. Whitaker Way Portland, Or. 97230 PH (503)254-9100 FAX (503)252-9508

WATERCOLOR BOOKS

Vol. 20	"Simply Country Watercolors" by Susan Scheewe Brown	257	$9.50 ___
Vol. 21	"Simply Watercolor" by Susan Scheewe Brown.....T.V. Book	260	$11.95 ___
Vol. 23	"Watercolor Step by Step" by Susan Scheewe Brown.....T.V. Book	294	$11.95 ___
Vol. 24	"Introduction to Watercolor" by Susan Scheewe Brown.....T.V. Book	314	$11.95 ___
Vol. 25	"Watercolors Anyone Can Paint" by Susan Scheewe Brown...T.V. Book	325	$11.95 ___
Vol. 26	"Watercolor - The Garden Scene" by Susan Scheewe Brown... T.V. Book	339	$11.95 ___
W Vol. 27	"Watercolor Landscapes" by Susan Scheewe Brown....T.V. Book	360	$11.95 ___
W Vol. 4	"Enjoy Watercolor" by Ellie Cook	210	$7.50 ___
Vol. 6	"Watercolor Memories" by Ellie Cook	246	$9.50 ___
Vol. 3	"Watercolor Made Easy 3" by Kathy George	301	$9.50 ___
Vol. 1	"The Way I Started" by Gary Hawk	120	$6.00 ___
Vol. 2	"Anyone Can Watercolor" by Ken Johnson	118	$6.50 ___
Vol. 1	"Watercolor Fun & Easy" by Beverly Kaiser	243	$7.50 ___
Vol. 1	"Flowers, Ribbon and Lace in Watercolor" by Linda McCulloch	280	$9.50 ___
Vol. 7	"Watercolor Charms" by Sharon Rachal...*NEW*	376	$9.50 ___

PEN & INK BOOKS / COLORED PENCIL BOOKS

Vol. 6	"Journey of Memories" by Claudia Nice	166	$6.50 ___
Vol. 7	"Scenes from Seasons Past" by Claudia Nice	183	$9.50 ___
Vol. 8	"Taste of Summer" by Claudia Nice	223	$9.50 ___
Vol. 9	"Familiar Faces" by Claudia Nice	284	$9.50 ___
Vol. 2	"Colored Pencil Made Easy" by Jane Wunder	242	$7.50 ___
Vol. 3	"The Beauty of Colored Pencil and Ink Drawing" by Jane Wunder	259	$7.50 ___
Vol. 4	"Watercolor, Pen and Ink" by Jane Wunder	357	$9.50 ___

VIDEOS BY SUSAN SCHEEWE BROWN

"Paintings For The Holidays" 1 Hour		$24.95 ___
"Fabric Painting Fun" 1 Hour		$24.95 ___
"Watercolor Techniques" 1 Hour	S8226	$19.95 ___
"Painting Projects" Watercolor 3 Hours	S8224	$49.95 ___
"Scheewe Art Workshop I" 13-1/2 HR Shows On 4 Tapes	S8225	$69.95 ___
"Scheewe Art Workshop II" 13-1/2 HR Shows On 4 Tapes	S8223	$69.95 ___

NAME ___________________________

____

ADDRESS ___________________________

____

CITY/STATE/ZIP ___________________________

____

PH( ) ___________________________

VISA ___________________________

M/C ___________________________

EXP. DATE ___________________________

SHIPPING $ ___________________________

SHIP TO ___________________________

____

____

——————— OILS BOOKS ———————

1	"His and Hers" by Susan Scheewe	101	$6.50 ___	
7	"Paint 'n Patch" by Susan Scheewe	107	$5.50 ___	
11	"I Love To Paint" by Susan Scheewe	111	$6.50 ___	
14	"Enjoy Painting Animals" by Susan Scheewe	114	$6.50 ___	
19	"Gift Of Painting" by Susan Scheewe O/AC/WC	230	$9.50 ___	
1	"Western Images" by Becky Anthony	186	$6.50 ___	
5	"Soft Petals" by Georgia Bartlett	171	$6.50 ___	
6	"Painting Fantasy Flowers" by Georgia Bartlett	215	$7.50 ___	
8	"Petals" by Georgia Bartlett	317	$9.50 ___	
9	"Floral Medley" by Georgia Bartlett *NEW*	344	$9.50 ___	
3	"Barnscapes & More" by Donna Bell	218	$9.50 ___	
4	"Countryscapes" by Donna Bell	249	$9.50 ___	
5	"Painter to Painter" by Donna Bell	263	$9.50 ___	
6	"Landscapes With Acrylics & Oil" by Donna Bell	282	$9.50 ___	
1	"Natures Palette" by Carol Binford.....O/AC	248	$9.50 ___	
2	"Oil Painting The Easy Way" by Bill Blackman	337	$9.50 ___	
3	"Lighted Windows & Gardens" by Bill Blackman...*NEW*	355	$9.50 ___	
1	"Mini Mini More" by Terri and Nancy Brown	150	$9.50 ___	
1	"Mini Mini More" by Terri and Nancy Brown	151	$9.50 ___	
4	"Heritage Trails" by Terri and Nancy Brown	169	$6.50 ___	
6	"Garden Trails" by Terri and Nancy Brown	283	$9.50 ___	
7	"More Garden Trails" by Terri and Nancy Brown...*NEW*	368	$9.50 ___	
2	"Windows of My World" by Jackie Claflin	181	$9.50 ___	
3	"Windows of My World 3" by Jackie Claflin	303	$9.50 ___	
4	"Windows Of My World 4" by Jackie Claflin...*NEW*	359	$9.50 ___	
4	"Expressions In Oil" by Delores Egger	239	$7.50 ___	
1	"Victorian Days" by Gloria Gaffney	240	$9.50 ___	
2	"Days of Heaven" by Gloria Gaffney	252	$9.50 ___	
6	"The Sky's The Limit" by Jean Green...*NEW*	372	$9.50 ___	

Vol. 3	"Nature's Beauty" by Bill Huffaker	177	$6.50 _	
Vol. 1	"In Full Bloom" by Susan Jenkins	313	$9.50 _	
Vol. 1	"Backroads of My Memory" by Geri Kisner	225	$9.50 _	
Vol. 2	"Backroads of My Memory" by Geri Kisner	245	$9.50 _	
Vol. 1	"Ducks and Geese" by Jean Lyles	172	$6.50 _	
Vol. 1	"Raining Cats & Dogs" by Todd Mallett	304	$9.50 _	
Vol. 1	"Pathway To Painting" by Lee McGowan	281	$9.50 _	
Vol. 2	"Another Path To Follow" by Lee McGowen	328	$9.50 _	
Vol. 1	"Bitterroot Backroads" by Glenice Moore-Nickel	330	$9.50 _	
Vol. 2	"Bitterroot Backroads 2" by Glenice Moore-Nickel	340	$9.50 _	
Vol. 3	"Bitterroot Backroads 3" by Glenice Moore-Nickel.*NEW*	369	$9.50 _	
Vol. 1	"Stepping Stones" by Judy Nutter	121	$6.50 _	
Vol. 1	"Painting with Paulson" by Buck Paulson	343	$11.95 _	
Vol. 1	"Rustic Charms" by Sharon Rachal	175	$6.50 _	
Vol. 2	"Rustic Charms II" by Sharon Rachal	199	$9.50 _	
Vol. 3	"Rustic Charms III" by Sharon Rachal	217	$6.50 _	
Vol. 4	"Rustic Charms IV" by Sharon Rachal	238	$7.50 _	
Vol. 5	"Rustic Charms V, Florals" by Sharon Rachal	261	$9.50 _	
Vol. 1	"Painting Flowers With Augie" by Augie Reis	152	$6.50 _	
Vol. 3	"Realistic Technique" by Judy Sleight	341	$9.50 _	
Vol. 2	"Soft & Misty Paintings" by Kathy Snider	229	$9.50 _	
Vol. 4	"Friends We've Known" by Gene Waggoner	187	$7.50 _	
Vol. 5	"Friends Are Forever" by Gene Waggoner	231	$7.50 _	
Vol. 1	"Fantasy Folk" by Don Weed	123	$6.50 _	
Vol. 2	"Painting The Clowns" by Don Weed	124	$6.50 _	
Vol. 1	"Something Special For Everyone" by Mildred Yeiser	158	$6.50 _	
Vol. 2	"Something Special For Everyone" by Mildred Yeiser	178	$6.50 _	
Vol. 5	"Soft & Gentle Paintings" by Mildred Yeiser	268	$9.50 _	

Susan Scheewe Publications, Inc.

ACRYLIC BOOKS

Vol. 19	"Gift of Painting" by Susan Scheewe	230	$9.50	
Vol. 1	"Painting It's Our Bag" by Bev Hink/Susan Scheewe	193	$9.50	
Vol. 4	"Keepsake Sampler" by Susan & Camille Scheewe	200	$9.50	
Vol. 1	"Loving You" by Susan & Camille Scheewe	244	$9.50	
Vol. 1	"Keepsakes For The Holidays" by Charleen Stempel & Susan Scheewe	286	$9.50	
Vol. 1	"Country Heartworks" by Reed Baxter	352	$9.50	
NEW Vol. 2	'Country Heartworks 2" by Reed Baxter	365	$9.50	
Vol. 1	"Kids And Water" by Joyce Benner	234	$9.50	
Vol. 2	"The Flower Market" by Joyce Benner	319	$9.50	
Vol. 1	"Country Fixin's" by Rhonda Caldwell	307	$9.50	
Vol. 2	"Country Fixin's - Sunflower Friends" by Rhonda Caldwell	321	$9.50	
Vol. 3	"Country Fixin's - For All Seasons" by Rhonda Caldwell	332	$9.50	
NEW Vol. 4	"Country Fixin's 4" by Rhonda Caldwell	364	$9.50	
NEW Vol. 1	"A Painters Garden" by Jane Dillon	354	$9.50	
Vol. 1	"Santas and Sams" by Bobi Dolara	258	$9.50	
Vol. 2	"Vintage Peace" by Bobi Dolara	270	$9.50	
Vol. 1	"Floral Designs" by Carol Empet	312	$9.50	
Vol. 2	"Floral Designs 2" by Carol Empet	338	$9.50	
NEW Vol. 3	"Floral Portraits" by Carol Empet	358	$9.50	
Vol. 1	"Romantically Tole Bauernmalerei" by Sherry Gall	311	$9.50	
Vol. 1	"Holiday Gathering" by Angie Hupp	267	$9.50	
Vol. 3	"Heavenly Gathering" by Angie Hupp	320	$9.50	
Vol. 1	"Happy Heart, Happy Home" by Cathy Jones	241	$9.50	
Vol. 1	"Pickets & Pastimes" by Marie & Jim King	329	$9.50	
Vol. 2	"Pickets & Pastimes 2, Heart of The Seasons" by Marie & Jim King	348	$9.50	
NEW Vol. 1	"For Me & My House" by Myrna King	370	$9.50	
Vol. 1	"Huckleberry Horse" by Hanna Long	269	$9.50	
Vol. 2	"Love Lives Here" by Mary Lynn Lewis	185	$6.50	
Vol. 3	"Love Lives Here" by Mary Lynn Lewis	195	$6.50	
Vol. 1	"Special Welcomes" by Corinne Miller	287	$9.50	
Vol. 2	"Special Welcomes" by Corinne Miller	298	$9.50	
Vol. 3	"Special Welcomes #3, Crazy About Crafting" by Corinne Miller	309	$9.50	
Vol. 4	"Special Welcomes #4 Farm-N-Friends" by Corinne Miller	324	$9.50	
Vol. 5	"Special Welcomes #5 All Wrapped Up" by Corinne Miller	333	$9.50	
Vol. 6	"Special Welcomes #6 Crop Keepers" by Corinne Miller	347	$9.50	
Vol. 1	"Change With The Seasons, Wire Loops" by Joanna Miller	331	$9.50	
Vol. 1	"Fruit & Flower Fantasies" by Joyce Morrison	277	$9.50	
Vol. 1	"Whimsical Critters" by Lori Ohlson	227	$7.50	
Vol. 2	"Sunflower Farm" by Lori Ohlson	326	$9.50	
Vol. 1	"Holiday Medley" by Nina Owens	265	$9.50	
Vol. 2	"Another Holiday Medley" by Nina Owens	296	$9.50	
Vol. 1	"Oh Those Little Rascals" by Diane Permenter	247	$9.50	
Vol. 6	"Acrylic Charms" by Sharon Rachal	305	$9.50	
Vol. 1	"Forever In My Heart" by Diane Richards.....AC/Fabric	188	$6.50	
Vol. 2	"Memories In My Heart" by Diane Richards.....AC/Fabric	189	$6.50	
Vol. 3	"Forever In My Heart II" by Diane Richards.....AC/Fabric	205	$9.50	
Vol. 6	"Angels In My Stocking" by Diane Richards	254	$9.50	
Vol. 7	"Nostalgic Dreams" by Diane Richards	273	$9.50	
Vol. 8	"Angel Kisses" by Diane Richards	346	$9.50	
NEW Vol. 1	"Country Fun For Chistmas" by Tina Rodriguez	367	$9.50	
Vol. 1	"Second Time Around" by Sally Sauermilch	297	$9.50	
Vol. 1	"Holiday Hangarounds" by Marsha Sellers	327	$9.50	
Vol. 1	"Creations In Canvas...and More" by Carol Spooner	256	$9.50	
Vol. 1	"Gran's Garden" by Ros Stallcup	295	$9.50	
Vol. 2	"Another Gran's Garden" by Ros Stallcup	315	$9.50	
Vol. 3	"Gran's Garden & House" by Ros Stallcup	334	$9.50	
Vol. 4	"Gran's Garden Party" by Ros Stallcup	345	$9.50	
NEW Vol. 4	"Gran's Treasures" by Ros Stallcup	363	$9.50	
Vol. 1	"Christmas Greetings from the Cottage" by Chris Stokes	336	$9.50	
Vol. 1	"Christmas Visions" by Max Terry	278	$9.50	
Vol. 3	"Painting Clay Pot-pourri" by Max Terry	310	$9.50	
NEW Vol. 4	"The Nesting Place" by Max Terry	373	$9.50	
Vol. 1	"Country Primitives" by Maxine Thomas	274	$9.50	
Vol. 2	"Country Primitives 2" by Maxine Thomas	300	$9.50	
Vol. 3	"Country Primitives 3" by Maxine Thomas	322	$9.50	
NEW Vol. 4	"Country Primitives 4" by Maxine Thomas	350	$9.50	
Vol. 1	"Rise & Shine" by Jolene Thompson	214	$6.50	
Vol. 2	"Garden Gate" by Jolene Thompson	250	$9.50	
Vol. 5	"Count Your Blessings" by Chris Thornton	213	$9.50	
Vol. 6	"Share Your Blessings" by Chris Thornton	226	$9.50	
Vol. 7	"Blessings" by Chris Thornton	255	$9.50	
Vol. 8	"Christmas Blessings" by Chris Thornton	266	$9.50	
Vol. 9	"Blessings For The Home" by Chris Thornton	275	$9.50	
Vol. 10	"Bazaar Blessings" by Chris Thornton	299	$9.50	
Vol. 11	"Painted Blessings" by Chris Thornton	323	$9.50	
Vol. 12	"Family Blessings" by Chris Thornton	349	$9.50	
NEW Vol. 13	"Garden Blessings" by Chris Thornton	356	$9.50	
NEW Vol. 14	"Friendship Blessings" by Chris Thorton	371	$9.50	
Vol. 1	"Watermelon Wedges and Rustic Edges" by Lorinne Thurlow	342	$9.50	
Vol. 2	"Watermelon Wedges and Rustic Edges 2" by Lorinne Thurlow	353	$9.50	
NEW Vol. 3	"Watermelon Wedges and Rustic Edges 3" by Lorinne Thurlow	362	$9.50	
Vol. 1	"Barnyard Friends" by Lou Ann Trice	306	$9.50	
NEW Vol. 1	"Farmer and Friends" by Lou Ann Trice	366	$9.50	
Vol. 5	"Daydreams & Sweet Shirts II" by Don & Lynn Weed	208	$9.50	
Vol. 1	"Connie's Favorite Old-Time Labels" by Connie Williams	335	$9.50	
NEW Vol. 2	"Connie's Garden Seed Packets" by Connie Williams	351	$9.50	
Vol. 1	"Floral Fabrics and Watercolor" by Sally Williams	262	$9.50	
Vol. 1	"A Time For Giving" by Evelyn Wright	308	$9.50	

Susan Scheewe
Publications, Inc.
13435 N.E. Whitaker Way
Portland, Or. 97230
Phone (503) 254-9100
Fax (503) 252-9508

* * * * * * *

SHIPPING &
HANDLING
CHARGES
Add $2.50 for the
First Book for shipping
and handling.

Add $1.50 per each
additional book.

Please Add $3.00 for
handling & postage.
PER TAPES. <u>Sorry we
must have a "NO RE-
FUND - NO RETURN"
policy.</u>

U.S CURRENCY

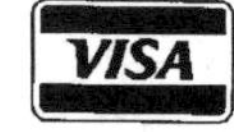 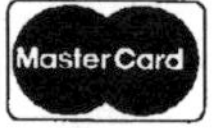

PRICES SUBJECT
TO CHANGE
WITHOUT NOTICE

FOR MORE
INFORMATION ON
BOOKS OR
SUPPLIES CALL OR
WRITE US

WE ARE ALWAYS
GLAD TO HEAR
FROM YOU!

12-20-96